THE PROMISE OF
AMERICAN LIFE

Memoirs of the
AMERICAN PHILOSOPHICAL SOCIETY
Held at Philadelphia
For Promoting Useful Knowledge
Volume 124

THE PROMISE OF AMERICAN LIFE

SOCIAL MOBILITY IN A NINETEENTH-CENTURY IMMIGRANT COMMUNITY, HOLLAND, MICHIGAN

1847–1894

GORDON W. KIRK, JR.

Associate Professor of History, Western Illinois University

THE AMERICAN PHILOSOPHICAL SOCIETY
Independence Square ● Philadelphia
1978

Library of Congress Catalog Card Number 78-50185
International Standard Book Number 0-87169-124-8
US ISSN 0065-9738

TO MY PARENTS

Acknowledgments

During the preparation of this manuscript, many people have generously given of their time and effort. I am particularly grateful to James H. Soltow for both his encouragement and helpful criticisms of several drafts of this work beginning at the dissertation level. In addition, Madison Kuhn, Robert P. Swierenga, and Clyde Griffin read all or parts of the manuscript, and their comments are deeply appreciated. Jerome M. Clubb provided both encouragement and valuable assistance in the analysis of the data in this investigation.

The research involved in this study required the generous assistance of many institutions and their staffs. To Richard Hathaway of the Michigan State Library for his help in locating various materials and for bending the rules to allow me to withdraw certain items, I am most appreciative. Likewise, Michael Traugott of the Inter-University Consortium for Political Research was most generous in assisting me in programming. In addition, the staffs of the Heritage Hall Collections at Calvin College, Hope College Library, Michigan State Archives, and The Netherlands Museum of Holland, Michigan, were most helpful.

A revised version of Chapter III co-authored with Carolyn Tyirin Kirk appeared in the *Journal of Social History* and is reproduced here with the editor's permission. Their cooperation is appreciated.

Without question, however, the greatest debt is owed to my wife, Carolyn, who endured much and made many sacrifices. Lovingly taking time out from her own work as a sociologist, she served as both research assistant and editor in the preparation of this manuscript for more years than either of us cares to remember. Perhaps even more importantly, she usually—but not always—listened to me ramble on about my work at all hours of the day and night. Perhaps the next time we can ramble on collectively about our joint project.

G. W. K., Jr.

CONTENTS

I. Introduction

ALTHOUGH theories and speculations regarding patterns and rates of social mobility underlie historical explanations of numerous social and political phenomena and contemporary students of social stratification continue to debate whether or not the American social order is becoming more or less rigid, until recently little systematic research on the mobility process in the nineteenth century has been conducted. This gap in our knowledge of mobility for the previous century underscores Lenski's point that not enough data are available to justify conclusions regarding changes in patterns and rates of mobility and that such data are a necessary prerequisite for a meaningful "discussion of the causes and consequences of shifts in rates of vertical mobility."[1] Given the lack of data over time and its importance to mobility theory, not only are more studies of nineteenth-century rates and patterns needed but also examinations analyzing both the effects of structural factors and changes on rates of movements and the relationship between vertical and horizontal movement are necessary for a fuller understanding of the mobility process.

Initial steps in this direction have been taken on a number of fronts. Elite studies dealing with the social origins of nineteenth- and early twentieth-century business leaders marked the first systematic effort to understand the social structure of the last century. The traditional view as expressed in the American dream had portrayed the background of the typical business leader as that of a poor farm boy or immigrant who rose to a position of prominence without the benefit of much education.[2] However, systematic analyses by Greg-

---

[1] Lenski, 1958: p. 514.
[2] For a discussion of this literature, see Miller, 1949: pp. 184–208.

1

ory and Neu of industrial leaders of the 1870's and by Miller of the business elite of the first decade of the twentieth century show that the overwhelming majority of the elite in both cases came from native upper- or middle-class backgrounds; by contrast, only a few such leaders were of working-class or immigrant origins.[3]

These first elite studies have since been supplemented by two other analyses of elite recruitment which have attempted to relate that phenomenon to broader changes in American society.[4] Examining the northeastern urban rich during the age of Jackson, Pessen questions many of the conclusions of De Tocqueville regarding the social fluidity of that period. In this age of alleged equality of opportunity, he finds both that few of the rich came from middling or lower classes and that the vast disparities between the urban rich and poor increased. In offering an explanation, Pessen suggests that these conditions were the result of the transportation revolution and the *de facto* national market it created which enhanced profit-making opportunities for those who already commanded a disproportionate share of "society's good things" at the expense of others. This plus "the massive internal migration, above all of younger, marginal persons of little standing, into and out of the nation's cities increased both the power and the share of wealth commanded by the more substantial and therefore more stable elements."[5]

On the other hand, Harris reaches somewhat different conclusions in comparing rates of elite recruitment over several centuries. Specifically, despite the apparent long-term constancy in elite recruitment, he argues that there has been, in fact, a cyclical pattern of elite recruitment on top of an overall trend towards greater equalitarianism. Related to short-term economic and demographic trends, furthermore, these patterns of recruitment tend to parallel Kuznet's cycles of long swings in the economy as well as being closely associated with immigration, population growth, and the settling of new communities. That is, he detects a pattern beginning with new waves of immigration followed by the creation of new towns coinciding with the beginnings of rapid spurts

---

[3] Gregory, and Neu, 1962: pp. 193–211 and Miller, 1962: pp. 329–358.
[4] Pessen, 1971: pp. 989–1034, and Harris, 1969: pp. 159–344.
[5] Pessen, 1971: pp. 989–1034.

in population and economic growth. In this process new communities generate new opportunities of many kinds through their needs for new political representatives, professionals, and merchants as well as farmers to develop virgin land. In essence then, increased mobility is a direct response to structural changes in the society—economic growth, population expansion, and the creation of new communities.[6]

Perhaps the most important contribution of these studies is pointing the direction that future research should take. Not only do they provide a backdrop for evaluating patterns of mobility but also they offer a number of fruitful hypotheses concerning the impact of structural factors that merit serious consideration whether the research focuses on the vertical movement of a particular occupational group or of a specific geographical area. The insights of Pessen regarding the impact of in- and out-migration and the development of the national market on patterns of mobility and the distribution of wealth need further examination by historians who undertake studies of mobility in the nineteenth century. Similarly Harris's conclusions concerning the impact of fluctuations in economic cycles, population growth, immigration, and the founding of new towns on the mobility process warrant serious attention if the forces producing various rates and patterns of mobility are to be more fully understood. In this connection, newly founded settlements need closer examination to determine whether or not the structural changes and characteristics in such communities foster patterns and rates of mobility that differ substantially from those found both after the "settlement period" has ended and in older, more established communities.

Although valuable, these elite studies do not give adequate answers to the question of mobility for the entire population. That is, it is possible to conceive of a society where both total self-recruitment of the elite exists and a high level of vertical mobility occurs throughout the rest of a society. The problem of the openness of a society, the fluidity of its social structure, and an understanding of the mobility process itself, therefore, is a far more complex problem than simply an appraisal of elite recruitment. In addition, it requires a com-

---

[6] Harris, 1969: pp. 218–252.

parative approach; only in this manner will it be possible
to isolate the significant variables affecting vertical movement.

Thus the examination of social mobility becomes a multi-
stage process. Initially, it entails a systematic examination
of mobility at all levels within the sample selected for study.
Next these findings need to be related to changes in the
occupational structure in order to determine to what extent
these changes affect rates of movement. Such an evaluation
further requires a consideration of the effects of the level
and rate of economic and demographic changes on the occupational structure. Then the observed rates of mobility must
be compared over space, that is, with studies in other places
during the same time period, in order to determine what
similarities and/or differences exist between communities
having different occupational structures and possessing different demographic, economic, technological, and environ-
mental characteristics. In addition, findings from the nineteenth century should be compared with those from other
time periods in order to gauge more fully the impact of chro-
nology and changing variables on the process of mobility.
This type of analysis will enable scholars to deal more ade-
quately with such questions as to whether or not the assumption of opportunity for the late nineteenth century is valid,
whether or not rates of vertical mobility are changing in
American society, what factors account for changes, which
structural patterns and changes yield the highest rates of
movement and what relationship exists between geographic
and occupational mobility. Answers to these questions will
lead to a fuller understanding of the effects of demographic
changes—urbanization, in- and out-migration, and population growth; economic changes—industrialism, the market
economy, and types of economic activity; and the frontier
on the fluidity of the nineteenth-century social order. A comparative analysis of this nature will not only offer insights
into the nature of nineteenth-century society but also lead
to the development of a more comprehensive theory of the
forces that affect the occupational structure and promote
fluidity in a social order.

The extant literature on nineteenth-century social mobility
is not yet sufficient to give precise answers to these questions.
One difficulty is that historians, unlike students of contempo-

rary society, do not have access to national samples of cross-sections of the American people. Moreover, given the state of the federal manuscript censuses and the available technology, the cost in dollars and manpower to draw such samples is prohibitive. However, less costly alternative strategies are available which promise equally fruitful results. A fuller understanding of nineteenth-century society can be attained through studies of numerous communities possessing different structural characteristics and undergoing various rates of change. Furthermore, making comparisons among these studies offers the possibility of isolating more fully the dynamic elements in the nineteenth-century American social order and the mobility process in general.

Like the elite studies, community studies of mobility represent another attempt to examine systematically the nineteenth-century social structure. Although these investigations are of great value, they are also marked by limitations that preclude a full understanding of the mobility process. With a few notable exceptions, the work thus far has tended to neglect structural and demographic characteristics, both changes and differences, among the communities studied. Almost all of them, falling into the category of the "new urban history" have focused attention on the differences in the mobility patterns of various racial and ethnic groups in medium-sized and large cities. Although the author of one of these studies has noted that "if historians are to understand occupational mobility they need to study . . . cities of various sizes and growth rates and with differing social and economic characteristics," little effort has been expended at making comparisons among these studies.[7] In fact, many of the mobility studies in adopting the label of the "new urban history," as one critic has suggested, reveal an impulse to limit their perspective and to avoid comparisons with rural or small urban settlements.[8] Consequently, the neglect of structural factors, the limitation of perspective, and the failure in many cases to provide meaningful comparisons among these studies have seriously limited our understanding of the mobility process in the nineteenth century.

In spite of these shortcomings, the extant literature has

---

[7] Hopkins, 1972: p. 218.
[8] Dykstra, 1971: p. 123.

also provided many valuable insights and marks a significant move in the direction of a clearer understanding of the American social order. The first study of occupational mobility in a nineteenth-century settlement was Curti's examination of Trempealeau County, Wisconsin, between 1850 and 1880. Selecting a frontier community with an ethnically heterogeneous population, his main purpose was "to apply objective tests to the Turner thesis about democracy" which Curti defines in part as involving the development of "equality of economic and cultural opportunity." According to Curti's interpretation of his data, "The rich became somewhat richer, the poor became a great deal less poor."[9]

Since Curti's study, the focus for the examination of nineteenth-century mobility has shifted markedly away from frontier communities to urban areas. This shift, which in part reflected the renewed interest of the historical profession in the city, perhaps may also be responsible for producing results contradictory to what Curti found to be true for Trempealeau County. Thernstrom's study of the unskilled laborers of Newburyport launched not only a whole new series of mobility studies but also offered a different picture of mobility in the nineteenth century. Using a medium-sized city in the years from 1850 to 1880 when both the economic and population growth of the community had leveled off and analyzing the careers of the unskilled laborers, who comprised 8 per cent of the labor force, he concludes that there was little in their experience to justify the concept of unlimited opportunity.[10]

Following these two initial studies, the subsequent examination of mobility has been confined to a number of urban areas. Included among these works are examinations of two large eastern cities, two medium-sized northern cities, and three southern cities. Blumin's study of ante-bellum Philadelphia marks one of the most serious attempts to relate mobility patterns to the changing economic structure of the city. In contrast to Curti, he argues the gap between the rich and the poor in ante-bellum Philadelphia widened. Finding that between 1820 and 1860 upward rates of occupational mobil-

---

[9] Curti, 1959: pp. 1, 445.
[10] Thernstrom, 1964: p. 114.

ity remained relatively constant while downward movement steadily increased, he argues that these patterns and the subsequent widening gap between the rich and the poor resulted from the reorganization of the labor force away from the craft shop and into the factory system.[11]

In addition to Philadelphia, mobility patterns in Boston have been examined by Knights and Thernstrom. As part of his extensive analysis of the growth of Boston, 1830–1860, Knights found that only in the 1850's did movement between the manual/non-manual line surpass 10 per cent and concludes that "success came to comparatively few." Looking at Boston from 1880 to 1968, Thernstrom finds that the higher rate found by Knights for the 1850's, with slight decadal variations, remained remarkably consistent in Boston after 1850. Perhaps more importantly, after comparing his findings regarding both intra- and inter-generational mobility with other studies, he suggests that the "post-1850 Boston pattern was manifested in a wide range of other cities." Part of this consistency he attributes to the similarity of the "averaged occupational structure" of different city size classes as indicated by 1950 data as well as the high level of geographic mobility in America. However, because cities with similar populations vary in structure and there is evidence that such variations may have been even greater in the nineteenth century, he indicates the need for "further study of such local variations and their consequences."[12]

Patterns of mobility have also been analyzed in two medium-sized northern cities, Poughkeepsie, New York, and Omaha, Nebraska. Using the former as an example of a less specialized small city with a more craft-oriented economy than that of a large industrialized urban area, Griffin investigated the differing mobility patterns of various ethnic and racial groups of that city. Comparing his findings with those of Thernstrom's study of Boston, he finds that blacks and Irish immigrants shared similar experiences of both low occupational status and mobility in both cities. However, the larger proportion of Germans in Poughkeepsie, who were also the most upwardly mobile immigrant group because they

---

[11] Blumin, 1969: pp. 165–208.
[12] Knights, 1971: pp. 96–102, and Thernstrom, 1973: pp. 232–241.

brought the requisite skills to the craft-oriented economy, gives the small New York City the impression of being more hospitable to immigrants than Boston.[13] In contrast to Poughkeepsie, Omaha represented a relatively new, rapidly growing, medium-sized city. Although downward movement into the blue collar category was low, Chudacoff finds that rates of upward mobility into white collar positions did not differ greatly from those of other cities and suggests that, in spite of its newness, Omaha had a relatively tight social structure.[14]

The remaining community mobility studies have focused on three southern cities of varying sizes and growth rates, Birmingham, Atlanta, and Galveston. As with many of the previous studies, the major question dealt with in these studies is whether or not various racial and ethnic groups enjoyed different rates of occupational and geographic mobility. Depending on the type of racial and/or ethnic classification employed, occupational mobility patterns indicate that whites were more mobile than blacks; native whites were more mobile than were immigrants who in turn enjoyed more success than blacks; and in Galveston, the pattern from high to low was native white, immigrants, Mexican-Americans, and blacks. Likewise the less successful groups also tended to fill a disproportionate number of positions at the bottom of the occupational hierarchy. Because of the concentration of these studies on the movement of various groups, however, little attention is devoted to the relationship of gross rates of mobility to broader social and economic changes taking place in these communities.[15]

If, as Lenski suggests, the central question in studying social stratification is "who gets what and why," the above works mark a major step towards answering the first part of that question.[16] These studies provide valuable information regarding relative rates of movement for various racial and ethnic groups and to a lesser degree for various occupational groups. The "why" part of the question, however, awaits

---

[13] Griffin, 1970: pp. 479–499.

[14] Chudacoff, 1972: pp. 96–110.

[15] Hopkins, 1968: pp. 200–213; Worthman, 1971: pp. 172–213; Barr, 1970: pp. 394–403.

[16] Lenski, 1966: p. 3.

further investigation and perhaps the raising of an additional question of how much overall mobility and why. A complete answer to the first question of who gets what and why may be dependent upon a fuller understanding of the broader structural question and focusing too much attention on the first may be analogous to putting the cart before the horse. That is, even more or at least equally as important as determining mobility differentials among various groups is the problem of understanding what structural characteristics yield what patterns and rates of mobility. Moreover, it is possible that the total amount of mobility affects the relative amount of movement enjoyed by various sub-groups. Such that, various minority groups rates of vertical movement may come closer to approaching the community's norm as the total amount of mobility in the community increases. Thus answering the question of how much and why may provide insights into the problem of who gets what and why. The paucity of occupational mobility studies for the nineteenth century and their general neglect of the impact of structural factors on the mobility process strongly indicate that more studies of vertical movement—and particularly studies focussing on structural changes and their sources—are needed before historians can provide adequate appraisals of changing rates of movement in American society, the mobility process in general, and the nature of nineteenth-century society.

II.

The purpose of this study is to examine social and geographic mobility in a small ethnically homogeneous community in western Michigan composed of the towns of Holland, Zeeland, and Holland township from its founding in 1847 to 1894. Focusing on economic and demographic changes, it will relate patterns of mobility in the Holland area to such changes and by comparing these findings with those of other examinations of mobility over time and space will seek to isolate the dynamic elements affecting the nineteenth-century social order. That is, the impact of population growth, geographic mobility, urbanization, industrialization, and the founding of new communities on the mobility process will be examined.

Like many of the small towns during the period under

consideration, the Holland area underwent a social and economic transformation. The area's population increased five-
fold between 1850 and 1890, jumping from 1,829 to 9,865
and the 1880's saw the population of the city of Holland
increase 50 per cent from 2,620 to 3,945. With this increase
in population and the beginnings of urbanization, an increasingly higher proportion of the labor force found employment
in the many small factories that arose in the area. The 1880
census of manufacturers reveals that 232 persons were employed in the community's factories which yielded an annual
product valued at $575,411. Twelve years later a business
compendium of Ottawa County reported that the industries
of Holland produced an annual output of over $2 million
and employed a thousand men.[17] Admittedly, economic
changes took place on a much smaller scale than in the large
urban centers that sprang up overnight in the Middle West.
Yet the changes occurring in Holland repeated themselves
in numerous communities throughout the nation.

This area, differing in many important respects from those
previously studied, typifies another type of community in
nineteenth-century America. Unlike both the ethnically heterogeneous large and medium-sized cities of the North and
South that have been studied and Curti's Trempealeau
County, Holland was an ethnically homogeneous frontier settlement that increasingly came to rely upon light industry
rather than agriculture. That the 1890 federal census reported over 45 million of a total population of 62 million
as residing in cities and towns with populations of less than
5,000 indicates that in size Holland represented the type
of community in America inhabited by over 70 per cent of
the population as late as the last decade of the nineteenth
century.[18]

The fact that Holland was initially settled by a group of
Dutch immigrants and consequently possessed a fairly homogeneous population also makes it representative of a large
number of nineteenth-century communities. In a large proportion, perhaps a majority, of towns, homogeneity rather
than heterogeneity was the norm. Johansen, in a suggestive

[17] Manuscripts of the *Tenth Census of the United States, 1880: Special Census of Manufac-turers.* Michigan State Archives and Mitchell, 1893: 1: p. 181.

[18] U.S. Department of Commerce, Bureau of the Census, *Historical Statistics of the United States, Colonial Times to 1957* (Washington, D.C., 1966), pp. 17–36.

essay, points out that within the context of the American experience migration has been largely a selective process. Stressing the pull factors rather than the push factors in migration theory, she argues that "migrants who choose one destination over an alternative of equal advantage have in common a range of value expectations which . . . are factors in the establishment of differentiated communities." The character of a community is thus determined by its first settlers and in "communicating their value satisfaction and dissatisfaction, they in effect, 'select' the migrants who will follow and thereby perpetuate the character of a differentiated community."[19] Moreover, Smith delineates two types of towns in the Midwest: those that were colonized as towns by relatively homogeneous ethnic and religious groups; and those which were not the result of any prior plan, with the former being far more important than historians have previously realized.[20]

The theory of Johansen and the work of Smith indicate that ethnic homogeneity was a common feature of many midwestern towns. A high proportion of Norwegian, Danish, German, Dutch, Swiss, Swedish, and British immigrants settled in rural counties. In 1890, for example, people of German origin constituted 75 per cent and 65 per cent respectively of people of Taylor and Dodge Counties in Wisconsin. Similarly, the Norwegians of Minnesota clustered in the southeastern part of that state. Many Dutch, Swedish, Danish, and Swiss followed parallel patterns of settlement. In forming ethnic enclaves many of the Germans, Dutch, and Scandinavians migrated as units. Within the Danish Lutheran Church, synodical reports frequently employed the phrase "gathering our people together" to mean gathering the people not only in church but also into settlements. Other ethnic groups expended similar efforts to encourage their fellow countrymen to join them. Migration to the Midwest was, then, a highly selective process which helped to foster and maintain many homogeneous communities.[21]

---

[19] Johansen, 1967: pp. 5–11.
[20] Smith, 1966: pp. 17–36.
[21] Stephenson, 1964: pp. 118–119; Faust, 1909: pp. 479–480; Qualey, 1938: p. 28; Lucas, 1955: *passim.;* Nyholm, 1963: p. 115. For a discussion of the location of other immigrant groups, see Johnson, 1951: pp. 1–41; Bergamn, 1958: *passim.;* Babcock, 1941: *passim.;* Degler, 1962: pp. 290–296.

In addition to their migration patterns, these immigrants supplied a significant portion of the total population of the country. Perusal of the federal census of 1890 makes this eminently clear by showing that the percentage of foreign-born and those native-born of foreign parentage in the states included in the North Atlantic region and the North Central division comprised 47 per cent and 43 per cent respectively of the population in those two sections. Although most of the major studies of immigrants have focused on the large numbers that concentrated along the eastern seaboard, new-comers to America as the above figures show and as Oscar Handlin has noted, "pushed their roots into many different soils."[22]

III.

It is important to examine social mobility in a community like Holland to understand more fully the nature of nine-teenth-century American society, and the available sources make such a study possible. As for almost all communities in the United States, the manuscripts of the federal census from 1850 to 1880 are available. These records provide a wealth of information on the occupational status and eco-nomic condition of all residents of the Holland community. Each census manuscript gives an enumeration of the popula-tion and the occupation of every employed person. The value of real estate holdings is also given in the census manuscripts for 1850, 1860, and 1870, and data on personal wealth are included in the manuscripts for 1860 and 1870.

The census of agriculture and the census of manufactures provide additional information regarding the economic con-dition of many people. The manuscripts of the census of agriculture from 1850 to 1880 give the value of farm land, equipment, and livestock. In addition, the manuscripts for 1870 and 1880 give the value of crops produced, wood cut, and livestock sold as well as the amount of wages paid to farm laborers. The census of manufactures provides detailed information about manufacturing concerns with a total an-nual value of production exceeding $500. Data on the amount

---

[22] The states of the North Atlantic division are Maine, New Hampshire, Vermont, Massachusetts, Rhode Island, Connecticut, New York, New Jersey, and Pennsylvania. Handlin, 1951: p. 144.

of capital, value of product, number of employees, wages paid, and the nature of the business are included within these manuscripts.

To supplement these sources, other valuable data for a mobility study of the Holland community exist. The most unique source is the emigration records from several of the provinces in The Netherlands. These records contain the name, religion, occupation, age, socio-economic status, and the reason for emigration for each head of household leaving the country between 1847 and 1876. Since many of these emigrants migrated to the Holland area, it is possible to compare their economic condition in The Netherlands with subsequent changes in America. The manuscripts from the Michigan state census of 1894 are also available for the city of Holland, making it possible to extend the mobility study of the city beyond 1880 to 1894.[23]

Using these various records makes it possible to trace the individual careers of all residents of the Holland community. The first step in setting up such a study was to develop a two-page questionnaire for all members of the male labor force that would encompass all relevant data from the census manuscripts. These data included name, birthplace, occupation, wife's and children's names and birthplaces, and ages of all household members which were converted to birth dates for convenience.[24]

Two major comparative methods were employed to link individuals both intra-generationally and inter-generationally. First, after recording all data from each of the censuses from 1850 to 1894, the forms were put in alphabetical order by census years in preparation for matching both individuals and fathers with sons. Among the problems encountered in this process were surname variations and individuals with the same name. In order to solve this problem, a list of surname variations was compiled to serve as a guide, i.e., Dykema and Diekema. Furthermore, to confirm matches,

---

[23] In addition to these sources, tax records and a county directory are accessible. However, in the former instance the data are in an unmanageable form, and in the latter case the information is not as complete as that in the state census of 1894.

[24] For an insightful essay on the process and problems of linking by name individuals enumerated in different censuses, see Winchester, 1970: pp. 107–125.

name, birth date, and birthplace of those in the labor force
and all members of their families were checked. For sons
who left home during the decade the problem of linkage
was more difficult. Matching these individuals with their fathers was accomplished by keeping a record of the last census
a son lived at home and then searching the following census
to see whether he was listed. Age was the major determinant
for distinguishing between similar names. Part of the problem
of tracing sons was alleviated since often they continued to
live with their parents after entering the labor force. Furthermore, sons who left home to raise a family frequently named
their first-born after the mother or father, depending on the
child's sex. Lastly, many of those who left home set up their
new residences next door to their parents.

The second comparison utilized the "addresses" of the
residents. That is, each census-taker numbered each household in order of enumeration. This information made it possible to make additional linkages by retracing the census-takers'
tracks. For example, all those linked between 1850 and 1860
were listed numerically by their 1860 number while all those
listed in 1850 only and 1860 only were arranged in two other
files by their respective enumeration numbers. When a pattern was found for a section of the 1850–1860 linked names
between routes taken by the two census takers—for example,
numbers 567–590 in 1850 corresponded closely to numbers
248–234 in Zeeland Township in 1860—gaps within that
range would be checked in the 1850 only and 1860 only
files to determine whether another linkage could be made
at that "address." As in the first method involving only
names, family information was utilized here. Both types of
comparisons were done several times in order to make as
many matches as possible. There were a few cases, however,
in which given all the information linkages seemed possible
but dubious; in these cases the two forms were not matched.
The number of such cases, however, was extremely small
and does not affect the general patterns found. Once this
matching was completed, the appropriate data from the censuses of agriculture and industry were added to the forms.
Then, those born in The Netherlands were checked against
the emigration records from that country.

Examining systematically patterns of occupational and

property mobility, this study will seek to relate these patterns of movement to demographic and economic changes in the Holland area. In this manner it will be possible to gauge more precisely the impact of these changes on the structural characteristics of the community, particularly its occupational structure, and in turn their effect on patterns and rates of mobility. In conjunction with this, the impact of in- and out-migration on the occupational structure and the relationship of these processes to occupational and property mobility will be closely examined. Lastly, the findings from Holland will be compared with data on occupational and geographic mobility from other studies of nineteenth- and twentieth-century communities. In pursuing this part of the analysis, data from these other studies will be reorganized and attention will focus on the differences in structural characteristics and changes among communities, in order to isolate more fully some of the dynamic elements in the American social order.

II. Background and Economic Development of the Holland Community

I.

LIKE many communities in the Middle West, the Holland settlement was a product of the increased immigration from Western Europe in the middle of the nineteenth century. A variety of social, economic, and religious factors provided the stimulus for migration to America and the establishment of a number of ethnic communities in the Middle West. Most writers have attributed the Dutch migration to the Middle West at this time to religious persecution in The Netherlands.[1] A close examination of the evidence, however, indicates that economic conditions provided the major stimulus for migration, while religion affected the pattern of settlement and the nature of the communities established.

The origins of the religious schism that played a role in the settling of the Holland community can be traced to religious reforms instituted by William I after the fall of Napoleon and the restoration of the monarchy. Calling for a reorganization of the State Church, William approved a new church constitution granting the throne powers traditionally held by the congregations or elected representatives of those bodies. Although maintaining the traditional divisions of church government—parish, consistory, classes, provincial boards, and synods—the constitution granted the king wide powers in the management of these bodies. Simultaneously with these governmental transformations, the church undertook a number of doctrinal changes resulting in a liberalization of church dogma. At first, only a small number of congregations left the national church in response to these changes.[2]

---

[1] See for example: Lucas, 1955: *passim.;* Pieters, 1923: *passim.;* Hyma, 1947: *passim.*
[2] Wabeke, 1944: pp. 84–88 and Lucas, 1955: pp. 42–43.

16

During the 1830's, however, an increasing number of clergymen began to voice opposition to these changes. Reverend Hendrick C. De Cock, the leader of this protest, quickly gained allies including the Reverends Albertus C. Van Raalte and Hendrick Peter Scholte, both of whom would later lead groups of Dutch emigrants to America. Opposition by these and others quickly gained the attention of both the crown and church officials. The expulsion of De Cock from the ministry by the latter group in 1834 precipitated a public secession from the church by De Cock and his congregation. Within a year Scholte, Van Raalte, and numerous other clergymen and their congregations joined the movement.[3]

For the next four years, government authorities sought with little success to eliminate the schism in the church. Church leaders called for the suppression of the dissidents and William I, determined to maintain his authority, rejected appeals by the Seceders for legal recognition. Instead, he ordered the fining and/or imprisonment of Secessionist ministers, disruption of meetings, and the quartering of soldiers in the homes of Seceders. This policy led to a stalemate. Efforts at suppressing the Seceders served only to strengthen the Movement and to weaken the State Church. On the other hand, fines and other punishments levied against splinter congregations proved burdensome to the dissenters. The resulting stalemate led to a religious settlement in 1838 whereby Seceders gained legal recognition subject to certain conditions. Henceforth, the government withheld recognition from and harassed only those congregations that proved unable to provide for their poor. The worst features of repression, moreover, ceased with the abdication of William in 1840, no incidents of repression occurred after 1846, and the last possibility of persecution ended with the adoption of a new and more liberal constitution in 1848.[4]

Occurring simultaneously with the religious turmoil was a worsening of economic conditions in The Netherlands in the 1830's and 1840's. The Belgian Revolution in 1830 and the refusal of William to comply with the conditions of separation drawn up by the great powers initiated a period of eco-

---

[3] Wabeke, 1944: pp. 84–89 and Lucas, 1955: pp. 42–53.
[4] Wabeke, 1944: pp. 88–92 and Lucas, 1955: pp. 44–53.

nomic stagnation. Adopting a policy of military resistance
to Belgian independence, the crown kept alive the threat
of war that necessitated the levying of high taxes in order
to maintain a large standing army. Moreover, the success
of the revolt denied Dutch commercial and shipping interests
access to Belgium's manufactured goods upon which trade
heavily depended while the policy of high taxation made it
difficult for Dutch manufacturers to expand and compete
abroad.[5]

Never fully recovered from these setbacks, the economy
experienced a major depression in the 1840's sparked by
the potato blight that swept over Ireland and other parts
of Western Europe. Virtually eliminating The Netherlands'
potato crop for two years, the blight in 1845 alone destroyed
over 160,000 acres of potatoes equivalent to 80 per cent
of the total output. The famine and the ensuing depression,
falling disproportionately on the middle and lower classes,
deprived many marginal farmers and laborers of their means
of earning a living at a time when industry was not expanding
sufficiently to absorb the excess labor supply. Unemployment
increased and the number of public charges rose from 13
per cent of the population in 1841 to 27 per cent by 1850.
The failure of the potato crop further resulted in food shortages. Many in the lower and middle classes, already unable
to afford meat and to secure bread because of shortages,
found themselves without an ample supply of cheap food.
These shortages frequently led to food riots which were forci-
bly suppressed.[6]

During the economic crisis, the government explored the
possibility of sending farmers to Surinam. Moved by the dis-
mal failure of this experiment, the government quickly aban-
doned any further plans for colonization. This change in
policy induced many private groups, including those led by
Van Raalte and Scholte to seek without success government
approval to establish colonies on the island of Java. With
the government's rejection of these proposals, attention
turned to America. The reputation America enjoyed as a
land of opportunity and the availability of cheap transporta-

---

[5] Wabeke, 1944: p. 87 and Lucas, 1955: pp. 53–56.
[6] Wabeke, 1944: pp. 91–92 and Lucas, 1955: p. 95.

tion from Western Europe further helps to explain this shift in focus.[7]

Consequently several groups organized and began to make preparations for emigration to the United States. While Scholte prepared to lead a band of settlers to Iowa, Van Raalte and Reverend Antonie Brummelkamp also considered the possibility of taking a group to America. Early in 1846, they organized a society and drew up a constitution inviting all who wished to join and emigrate as a Christian colony. Although the constitution did not exclude non-Seceders, Seceders constituted the majority of the organization. Later that year, Van Raalte and a small group of his followers departed for the United States. After several months of investigation and consultation with ministers and friends of the Dutch Reformed Church in America, Van Raalte decided to locate his colony in Ottawa County on the Black River twenty-five miles northwest of Grand Rapids in western Michigan. After purchasing a large tract of land for that purpose, he wrote Brummelkamp of his decision and requested that he, Brummelkamp, encourage members of the society and other potential emigrants to join the colony.[8]

Van Raalte's group was part of a general migration from the Netherlands in the 1840's and 1850's. In this migration, religion and religious issues served more as an organizing mechanism than as a stimulant to migration. Following the pattern characteristic of Roman Catholics and other Seceders from The Netherlands, Van Raalte and his followers chose to migrate and settle as a group in contrast to members of the State Church who displayed a greater propensity to migrate as families or individuals.[9]

Religious suppression, however, did not play a major role in the decision to migrate. As has been pointed out, the harshest aspects of persecution had ended by at least 1840, and the last instance of repression occurred in 1846. Thus by the second half of the 1840's when the large migration from The Netherlands began, the religious situation had improved greatly. Secessionist leaders of the migration, like Scholte, moreover, did not consider "present obstruction

---

[7] Wabeke, 1944: p. 95 and Lucas, 1955: pp. 56–59.

[8] Wabeke, 1944: pp. 115–117 and Lucas, 1955: pp. 68–76.

[9] Wabeke, 1944: pp. 114–115.

of worship a valid reason for leaving the fatherland."[10] Likewise, Van Raalte and Brummelkamp sought at first to remain
under the authority of the Dutch crown by migrating to Java
where the likelihood of religious difficulties with the official
church and crown would be greater than in America. In their
pamphlets expounding the advantages of migration they
elected not to emphasize religious persecutions but the economic gains of such a step.[11]

Data gathered by the Dutch government and published
in the *Staatcourant* in 1848 also indicate that economic conditions provided the major stimulus to migration. These data
reveal that the Seceders did not comprise the largest religious
group leaving the country and that religious freedom was
not the main reason for emigration. During 1847, the year
of the largest out-migration, only 653 of the 2,294 heads
of family or single people leaving The Netherlands classified
themselves as Seceders. The majority of the emigrants, 1,189,
claimed membership in the Hervormde Kerk or State Church
while Roman Catholics with 452 emigrants comprised the
third largest group. In addition, of the people leaving The
Netherlands in 1847, only 439 listed the desire for religious
freedom as one of their reasons for departing while an even
smaller number, 149, gave this as their sole reason for
leaving.[12] Furthermore, there is no evidence to suggest that
those desiring religious freedom were exclusively part of the
group settling in the Holland community. Of the immigrants
leaving the province of Groningen before 1850, thirty-two
could be positively identified as settling in the Holland community. Out of this admittedly small sample, only five cited
religion as one of the reasons for their migration while
twenty-five claimed that they left solely for economic
reasons.[13] From this small sample and the data for all migrants in 1847, it would appear that economic reasons provided the impetus for Dutch emigration while religion influ-
enced the pattern of settlement.

[10] *Ibid.*, pp. 89–90.

[11] Antonie Brummelkamp and Albertus C. Van Raalte, "An Appeal to the Faithful
in the United States of North America, May 25, 1846," in Lucas (ed.), 1955: **I**:
pp. 14–20.

[12] Cited in Wabeke, 1944: pp. 89–90.

[13] Emigration Records, The Netherlands, 1848–1876, Calvin College, Heritage
Hall Collection. Figures compiled by the author.

II.

After purchasing over 5,000 acres of land from the state of Michigan, Ottawa County, and private citizens with the funds of the Society, his own money, and that which he was able to raise in America, Van Raalte made final preparations in January, 1847, for the establishment of the colony. His overall goal for the community entailed more than a simple migration of people. He hoped both to promote the economic advancement of his people and to establish a Christian community.[14]

The following months witnessed the establishment of the colony and the steady arrival of new immigrant families. That same year under the leadership of Jannes Van De Luyster, a prosperous Dutch businessman, and Reverend Cornelius VanDer Meulen, a group from the province of Zeeland started a new settlement by that name within the colony. Other groups of immigrants followed this pattern and named new communities after their provinces of origin in The Netherlands such as Drenthe and Groningen. Viewing these developments as necessary for the success of the colony, Van Raalte strongly encouraged other groups of immigrants to settle either in or near his settlement in order to fulfill his ambition of establishing a strong Christian community.[15]

For the Holland community, the years from 1847 to 1894 witnessed dramatic changes in the size of its population and the development of its economic life. Both the expansion of agricultural and particularly industrial production far exceeded the five-fold increase in population recorded between 1850 and 1890. In addition, as a result of transportation improvements manufacturing turned from the simple processing of natural resources and agricultural products for consumption within the community to the production of consumer and producer goods for regional and national markets as well as for local consumption. With these economic changes, the occupational structure underwent major changes as the number of non-agricultural occupations increased.

---

[14] Hyma, 1947: pp. 120–127; Van Koevering, n.d.: pp. 295–296, 306.

[15] Lucas, 1955: pp. 110–141 and Hyma, 1947: p. 114. These townships and villages are included in the analysis of mobility in the Holland community.

By 1890, the population of the Holland community had grown to 9,865—more than five times larger than in 1850 (see table 1). By that year the settlement included Holland Township, the city of Holland, Zeeland Township, and the village of Zeeland which was a part of the latter township. The more than five-fold expansion of the population can be divided into two periods. Very rapid growth characterized the period to 1870 while the years following 1870 witnessed a more modest growth in population; population growth exceeded 80 per cent in the two decades prior to 1870 and never surpassed 20 per cent in the two following decades. At the same time more concentrated centers were established. In 1867 the city of Holland was incorporated and by 1880 the village of Zeeland was noted in the census. A comparison of the three major divisions indicate that, although the city of Holland expanded at a lower rate than the two townships

TABLE 1

POPULATION GROWTH OF THE HOLLAND COMMUNITY, 1850–1890

	City[a] of Holland	Zeeland[b] Township	Holland Township	Total Holland Community
1850:				
Population			1,829	1,829
1860:				
Population		1,466	1,891	3,357
Percentage Increase			3.4	83.6
1870:				
Population	2,319	2,343	2,353	7,015
Percentage Increase		59.8	24.4	108.9
1880:				
Population	2,620	2,715 (484)[c]	3,064	8,399
Percentage Increase	13.0	15.9	30.2	19.7
1890:				
Population	3,945	2,834 (785)[c]	3,086	9,865
Percentage Increase	50.6	4.4	0.7	17.5

[a] The city of Holland was incorporated in 1867.
[b] Zeeland Township became legally separated from Holland Township in 1851.
[c] Zeeland village; also included in totals for Zeeland Township.

Source: U.S., Department of Commerce, Bureau of the Census, *Eleventh Census of the United States, 1890: Population* 1: p. 221.

in the 1870's, the population of the townships increased only slightly in the 1880's while the city began a period of rapid expansion.

In spite of this rapid population growth, the community's ethnic composition as indicated by the adult male labor force remained intact. Dutch immigrants or their offspring continued to comprise the overwhelming majority of the labor force thus fulfilling Van Raalte's vision of a homogeneous community (see table 2). Although a steadily declining majority, the Dutch-born comprised the majority of the labor force from 1850 to 1880, representing over 90 per cent of the labor force in the first two decades before declining to 83.3 and 61.8 per cent in 1870 and 1880 respectively. The addition of many native-born sons of Dutch immigrants to the labor force in large part accounts for the decreasing proportion of Dutch-born workers. For example, of the 543 workers in 1880 born in the North Central states, 429 or 79.1 per cent of them were of Dutch immigrant parentage. The combined total of Dutch immigrants and their sons thus equaled 82.1 per cent of the community's labor force in 1880 and suggests that the decrease in the proportion of Dutch-born workers did not represent a significant decline in the homogeneity of the community.

TABLE 2

Ethnic Composition of the Holland Labor Force, 1850–1880[a]

Place of Birth	1850		1860		1870		1880	
	No.	%	No.	%	No.	%	No.	%
Netherlands	547	97.3	951	92.2	1,258	83.3	1,308	61.8
North Central States	1	0.2	10	1.0	66	4.4	543	25.7
New England	4	0.7	7	0.7	14	0.9	15	0.7
Mid-Atlantic States	4	0.7	37	3.6	99	6.6	120	5.7
Other U.S.	1	0.2	0	0.0	2	0.1	4	0.2
Western Europe	4	0.7	22	2.1	40	2.6	72	3.4
English-Speaking Countries	1	0.2	4	0.4	31	2.1	53	2.5
Eastern Europe	0	0.0	0	0.0	0	0.0	0	0.0
Unknown	0	0.0	0	0.0	0	0.0	1	0.0

[a] The manuscripts of the 1890 U.S. Census are not available and those for the 1894 state census exist only for the city of Holland.

Source: Manuscripts of the U.S. Censuses, 1850–80. Percentages calculated by the author.

An influx of non-Dutch migrants into the community, however, accounted for a part of the decline in the proportion of Dutch-born workers. Persons born in the North Central states, Mid-Atlantic states, primarily New York, and other immigrant groups from Western Europe, particularly Germany, steadily increased their proportion of the labor force. Thus, by 1880 native-born residents of non-Dutch parentage comprised 12.0 per cent of the labor force, while immigrants from Western Europe and English-speaking countries totaled almost 6 per cent of the labor force. Nevertheless, the community as indicated by the labor force largely maintained the ethnic homogeneity intended by its founder.

This homogeneity prevailed not only because of the continuous influx of Dutch immigrants into the community but also because of the greater reluctance of this group to migrate out of the community. Generally non-Dutch members of the labor force displayed a greater propensity to leave than did their Dutch counterparts. Between 1870 and 1880, 57 per cent of those born in The Netherlands remained in the community's labor force compared with only 32.4 per cent of the non-Dutch born. Within this latter group, only other immigrants from Western Europe with a rate of 47.5 per cent remaining came close to matching the persistence rate of the Dutch-born population.

While experiencing rapid population growth, the Holland community underwent even greater economic development in the years from 1847 to 1894. Intricately related to this development were transportation improvements linking the community to both regional and national markets. Clearly recognizing that the prosperity of the settlement depended on access to markets, the early settlers energetically sought improved transportation facilities for the community. Furthermore, as was true throughout nineteenth-century America, federal and state governments played major roles in providing these improvements. The first major step toward tying the colony to regional markets came in 1848 when the state of Michigan granted 4,000 acres of land to Kent, Allegan, and Ottawa counties for internal improvements with the stipulation that roads built between the towns of Allegan, Grand Haven, and Grandville, a small town outside of Grand Rapids, "be terminated at such point or points within the limits of the . . . Holland colony as shall be deemed most conducive to the interest of the said colony. . . ."[16]

Utilizing Black Lake which linked the colony to Lake Michigan offered even greater transportation rewards than did the construction of roads. Although large enough to accommodate any vessel sailing on the Great Lakes, the lack of docking facilities at Holland and the natural obstructions presented by the sand bars in the channel connecting Black Lake to Lake Michigan prohibited extensive use of this route. A combination of local initiative and state and federal aid in the form of land grants and direct cash subsidies during the 1850's led to both the clearing of the channel and the construction of docking facilities which guaranteed the future usefulness of Black Lake as a vital artery for the colony to Great Lakes traffic.[17]

More importantly, by 1870 three small railroad lines, the Michigan and Ferrysburg, the Holland and Allegan, and the Holland and Grand Haven serviced the area. With these lines and the completion of the Grand Rapids to Holland line by the West Michigan Railroad the following year, the community enjoyed daily freight and passenger service to Detroit, Chicago, and Kalamazoo. Thus by the beginning of the 1870's, the combination of lake and rail transportation had connected the Holland community to both regional and national markets which further facilitated the economic development of the settlement.[18]

With the expansion of population and the incorporation of the community into regional and national transportation systems, both the industrial and agricultural sectors of the economy recorded high per capita growth rates. There were differences in these two sectors however. Specifically, the agricultural sector grew much more rapidly before 1870 than in the decades following. In contrast, industrial output surpassed that of agriculture with its highest rate of per capita growth coming after 1870. Not only did the industrial sector grow rapidly but also manufacturing gradually turned from the processing of natural resources and agricultural products

---

[16] Lucas, 1955: p. 261.
[17] VanderVeen, 1911: p. 27 and Lucas, 1955: pp. 261–265.
[18] Lucas, 1955: pp. 286–287.

for local consumption to producing more goods for export
from the community.

Information compiled from the manuscripts of the federal
censuses and published data in the state censuses illustrates
the rapid development of the industrial sector. The federal
censuses, listing every establishment with an annual product
in excess of $500, indicate that production increased at a
rate fifteen times faster than the community's population between 1850 and 1880 (see table 3). Within each of the three
decades, moreover, gains in industrial production far outstripped those in population expanding over three times
more rapidly than population in the first two decades and
over ten times more rapidly in the 1870's.

Likewise data from the state censuses reveal high rates
of growth (see table 4). Industrial output almost tripled in
the decade following the state census of 1854 and the ten
years following 1864 witnessed a spectacular eight-fold increase in production while population rose 74 per cent. Although omitting data for the value of production for 1884
and 1894, the state censuses include information on the
amount of capital invested in industry which offers some indication of industrial development. The slight increase in capital between 1874 and 1884 which seemingly contradicts the
magnitude of change reported in the federal census results
from changes in the method of taking the state census in
1884 rather than a decline in industrial growth. Collecting
information for only seven selected industries, this proce-
dural change in the 1884 census resulted in the exclusion
of a number of industries and companies existing in the Holland community such as the Cappon and Bertsch tannery
reported by the federal census taker in 1880 as having a
total capital investment of $90,000. Moreover, omissions in
the 1884 state census, while diminishing the amount of
change occurring between 1874 and 1884, magnify increases
taking place in the decade following 1884. Thus the state
census of 1894 reports more than a five-fold increase in capital invested in industry between 1884 and 1894, in part, because the 1894 census like that in 1874 includes a far more
comprehensive enumeration of industry than its predecessor.
A comparison of data for 1874 and 1894, moreover, indicates
that there was substantial industrial progress in this twenty-

TABLE 3

INDUSTRIAL AND POPULATION GROWTH OF THE HOLLAND COMMUNITY AS RECORDED IN THE FEDERAL CENSUSES, 1850–1880.

Year	Number of Establishments	Capital	Number of Employees	Value of Production	Per Cent Increase	Population	Per Cent Increase
1850	3	$ 9,600	19	$ 18,560	. . . .	1,828	. . . .
1860	11	36,800	46	79,870	330%	3,457	84%
1870	74	218,300	194	347,758	335%	7,015	109%
1880	59	616,312	483	1,063,942	206%	8,399	20%
Total Change	56	606,712	464	1,035,582	5,585%	6,571	359%

Source: Manuscripts of the Seventh Census of the United States, 1850: Manufacturers of the United States; Manuscripts of the Eighth Census of the United States, 1860: Manufacturers of the United States; Manuscripts of the Ninth Census of the United States, 1870: Census of Industry and Wealth; Manuscripts of the Tenth Census of the United States, 1880: Manufacturers of the United States, Michigan State Archives.

TABLE 4

INDUSTRIAL AND POPULATION GROWTH OF THE HOLLAND COMMUNITY AS RECORDED
IN THE STATE CENSUSES. 1854–1894

Year	Number of Establish- ments	Capital Invested	Value of Pro- duction	Per Cent Increase	Popu- lation	Per Cent Increase
1854	16	$ 17,000	$ 20,180	. .	1,897	. .
1864	9	27,400	58,660	181%	4,470	136%
1874	18	210,000	470,500	702%	7,761	74%
1884	20	211,800	. .	. .	8,972	16%
1894	60	1,181,226	. .	. .	12,500	39%

Source: Michigan Department of State, *Census & Statistics of the State of Michigan,
1854,* pp. 287–291; Michigan Department of State, *Census & Statistics of the State of
Michigan, 1864,* pp. 457–461; Michigan Department of State, *Census of the State of
Michigan, 1874,* pp. 543–556; Michigan Department of State, *Census of the State of
Michigan, 1884: Agriculture and Manufactories,* **2**: pp. 312–396; Michigan Department
of State, *Census of the State of Michigan, 1894: Agriculture, Manufactories, Mines and
Fisheries,* **2**: pp. 574–873.

year period; industrial investment increased at a rate over
seven times that of population, 462 per cent compared to
61 per cent.

While industrial data from both the federal and state censuses indicate substantial growth, reasons exist for question-
ing this evidence and modifying conclusions drawn from it.
Home industry no doubt comprised an important source of
production during the early years of the settlement. As the
economy of the community became more specialized and
complex, however, it is reasonable to assume that such activity declined. Consequently, the available industrial data which
omit this activity will overestimate growth rates since this
unreported productivity would no doubt be greater in the
base years than in subsequent years. These weaknesses in
the data, however, do not deny the conclusion that gains
in industrial production far outstripped those in population
and that the most significant per capita gains took place after
1870.

Omissions in the recording of industrial information offers
another potential source of error. Since the census of manufacturing was coincidental to the enumeration of the population and only fifteen cents was paid for each establishment
recorded, the census taker received little incentive to do a

thorough job. Consequently, although every establishment with an annual product in excess of $500 was to be recorded, the census taker might not have made a special return trip to an establishment omitted in his original canvass of the population.[19] As a result, more manufacturing units might be recorded in some census years than in others owing to the diligence of the census taker which, in turn, might affect observed growth rates.

This, however, neither accounts for the decline in the number of businesses from 73 in 1870 to 59 in 1880 nor necessitates additional qualification of the industrial growth rates delineated from census materials. Of the 73 establishments enumerated in 1870, 51 had disappeared by 1880 while 37 new ones were reported. The mobility patterns of those businessmen listed in 1870 and remaining for the next enumeration do not indicate that the 1880 industrial census omitted large numbers of businessmen. Forty-eight of the 79 businessmen (many of the firms were partnerships which explains why there are more businessmen than business establishments) retained the same occupational position and 14 others entered either the professional or farm operators category. By contrast 17 became blue-collar workers. Those entering manual positions offer the best indication of potential omissions in the industrial census; that is, skilled workers operating small shops would most likely be omitted in this census. However, that only 9 of the 17 were listed as skilled workers does not indicate major omissions occurred. A more likely explanation for these data on the changing number of business establishments is that "easy entry and easy exit" characterizes firms in new communities just as it does firms in new industries.

During this period, dramatic changes in the community's industrial activity accompanied rapid economic growth. Manufacturing gradually turned from the simple processing of natural resources and agricultural products for local markets to the more sophisticated production of consumer and producer goods for export. In the first two decades under consideration the milling of lumber and grain dominated the com-

---

[19] U.S. Department of Commerce, Bureau of the Census, *Ninth Census of the United States, 1870: Census of Industry and Wealth* (Washington, D.C., 1870), pp. 337–338.

munity's industrial activity. All three of the manufacturing enterprises, two sawmills and a pearl ash factory, listed in 1850 exploited the most readily available natural resource of the community. The 1860 census indicates a slight diversification in economic activity; in addition to those industries previously enumerated, two tanneries, a boot and shoe factory, two tin shops, and two fishing companies are also listed.[20]

With the coming of the railroad to the Holland community in the late 1860's as well as more efficient lake transportation which facilitated the marketing of the community's industrial and agricultural products, the economy not only continued to grow but also concentrated increasingly on the production of finished goods for both local and regional markets. The 1860's witnessed the establishment of a number of small factories manufacturing sashes and doors, wagons, harnesses, metal products, clothing, saddles, furniture, and pumps. Even with these changes, however, the bulk of the industrial activity still serviced an agricultural economy; the largest enterprises remained flour and saw milling with the two largest mills producing an annual product in excess of $80,000.[21]

A broader transformation in industrial activity took place during the 1870's than in the previous two decades. Although milling remained important and the area maintained various farm-related industries, e.g., wagon-making, cooperage, harness-making, etc., for local rural consumption, industries producing goods for local non-farm residents and for export became even more important. Food processing firms—other than grain mills which continued to increase—including several meat-packing firms, a cheese and butter factory, and a bread factory, were established while leather-processing came to dominate the community. By 1880 the tanneries of the community had a combined total product of $621,795 accounting for almost 60 per cent of all industrial output, the bulk of which found markets outside the community.[22]

---

[20] Manuscripts of the *Seventh Census of the United States, 1850: Manufacturers of the United States* and Manuscripts of the *Eighth Census of the United States, 1860: Manufacturers of the United States*, Michigan State Archives.

[21] Manuscripts of the *Ninth Census of the United States, 1870: Manufacturers of the United States*, Michigan State Archives.

[22] Manuscripts of the *Tenth Census of the United States, 1880: Manufacturers of the United States*, Michigan State Archives.

Between 1880 and 1894, industrial activity both continued to expand and became increasingly specialized. Accompanying these developments was the concentration of activity within the boundaries of the city of Holland which paralleled the growing population there. Of the community's fifty-two industrial concerns enumerated in the state census of 1894, forty-four were located in the city of Holland whereas the previous state census listed only half of the twenty concerns in seven selected industries there.[23] Part of the growth and changes in economic activity during these years was due to the flow of outside capital into the area resulting in the establishment of both the C. L. King basket factory employing 200 men and the West Michigan Furniture Company.[24] By 1894, moreover, furniture manufacturing and leather processing dominated the economic life of the community. The four furniture companies employed almost 600 persons and possessed a combined capital of $300,000. Related industries manufacturing wood products possessed a capital investment of over $225,000 and employed 268 workers. In addition, Holland's two largest tanneries accounted for $305,000 worth of capital and employed 250 people.[25]

The available agricultural information, unfortunately, is not as extensive as that for manufacturing, thus allowing only tentative estimates of growth. Only in 1870 and 1880 did the federal census record the value of agricultural production, while the state of Michigan collected similar data in only 1884 and 1894. That farm prices declined sharply after 1870 further complicates the assessment of rates of agricultural development. However, the state censuses taken between 1854 and 1894 supply additional indicators of agricultural development in the form of data pertaining to acreage and the production of both staple crops and livestock which makes possible some estimate of long-range trends in agricultural development.

Although displaying substantial growth, the agricultural

[23] Michigan Department of State, *Census of the State of Michigan, 1884: Agriculture and Manufactories* (2 v., Lansing, Mich., 1885) **2**: pp. 312–396 and Michigan Department of State, *Census of the State of Michigan, 1894: Agriculture, Manufactories, Mines and Fisheries* (2 v., Lansing, Mich., 1895) **2**: pp. 574–873.

[24] *Holland City News*, August 3, 1890, and Potts, 1893: **2**: p. 49.

[25] Michigan Department of State, *Census of the State of Michigan, 1894: Agriculture, Manufactories, Mines, and Fisheries* (Lansing, Mich., 1895) **2**: pp. 574–873.

sector, as indicated by the above sources, did not expand
as rapidly as manufacturing, and, in contrast to the industrial
sector, agriculture grew much more rapidly before the 1870's
than after. Information pertaining directly to agricultural
production from both the state and federal censuses reveal
a sharp decline in the value of total output after 1870; the
value of agricultural production fell over 50 per cent between
1870 and 1883 (see table 5). Even when agricultural prices
are adjusted to a constant value based upon 1870 prices,
the decline in the value was still 46 per cent. Following this
precipitous decline during the 1870's and early 1880's, the
value of agricultural production rose 32 per cent by 1893,
still far below the level achieved in 1870. Even taking into
consideration declining prices, production in 1893 did not
regain its 1870 level; adjusting prices to 1870 levels the value
of agricultural output in 1893 equaled only 80 per cent of
that for 1870.

Such figures, however, offer only a partial picture of the
agricultural development of the community. A perusal of
other indicators of agricultural development suggests that
farming in the Holland community displayed sizable growth
between 1854 and 1874 before leveling off to more modest
rates of increase between 1874 and 1894 (see table 6). Improved acreage, for example, increased four-fold between
1854 and 1874 and then redoubled in the next twenty years.

Information pertaining to crop production similarly reveals

TABLE 5

SELECTED FIGURES RELATED TO THE AGRICULTURAL DEVELOPMENT OF THE HOLLAND
COMMUNITY, 1870–1894

Year	Value of Production	Per Cent Change	Value in 1870 Prices	Per Cent Change	Agriculture Price Level	Per Cent Change
1870	$511,490	. .	$511,490	. .	.483	. .
1883	244,507	−52%	277,515	−46%	.418	−13.5%
1893	321,880	32%	403,215	85%	.361	−13.6%

Source: Manuscripts of the Ninth Census of the United States, 1870: Census of
Agriculture, Michigan State Archives; *Census of the State of Michigan, 1884: Agriculture
and Manufactories,* **2**: pp. 312–396; *Census of the State of Michigan, 1894: Agriculture,
Manufactories, Mines and Fisheries* **2**: pp. 574–873; U.S. Department of Commerce,
Bureau of the Census, *Historical Statistics of the United States, Colonial Times to 1957*
(Washington, D.C., 1960), pp. 267–68.

TABLE 6
Agricultural Development of the Holland Community, 1854–1894

Year	Improved Acres	Per Cent Increase	Total Acres	Per Cent Increase	Acres of Corn	Percentage of Improved Acres Used for Corn	Per Cent Increase	Bushels of Corn	Per Cent Increase	Acres of Wheat	Percentage of Improved Acres Used for Wheat	Per Cent Change	Bushels of Wheat	Per Cent Increase
1854	5,381	··	39,906	··	1,320	24.5	··	30,321	··	362	6.7	··	7,114	··
1864	12,826		30,381	-6%	1,706	13.3		32,966	8%	2,246	17.4		27,396	285%
1874	21,130		58,667	101%	3,949	18.7		105,844	221%	4,099	19.4		55,704	103%
1884	36,139		49,775	8%	3,780	10.5		21,672	-80%	6,555	18.4		58,810	6%
1894	40,730		46,006	48%	4,602	11.3		107,457	396%	5,369	13.2		76,831	31%

Year	Bushels Other Grain	Per Cent Increase	Tons of Hay	Per Cent Increase	Pounds Butter	Per Cent Change	Horses	Per Cent Change	Oxen	Per Cent Change
1854	17,446	··	265	··	30,791	··	36	··	304	··
1864	16,414	-6%	4,097	1446%	83,860	173%	532		431	42%
1874	33,010	101%	5,220	22%	206,151	146%	980		188	-57%
1884	35,783	8%	3,797	-37%	295,592	33%	1,547		85	-55%
1894	53,010	48%	8,960	136%	327,196	11%	2,221		10	-88%

Year	Milch Cows	Per Cent Change	Sheep	Per Cent Change	Swine	Per Cent Change	Per Cent Population Change
1854	503	··	··		1,083	··	··
1864	1,444	187%	437		1,559	119%	136%
1874	2,268	57%	958	119%	1,052	27%	74%
1884	3,119	38%	1,217	27%	2,496	-6%	16%
1894	2,927	-6%	1,143		2,803		132%

Source: *Census & Statistics of the State of Michigan, 1854*, pp. 284–287; *Census & Statistics of the State of Michigan, 1864*, pp. 453–456; *Census of the State of Michigan, 1874*, pp. 270–392; *Census of the State of Michigan, 1884: Agriculture and Manufactories* 2: pp. 2–309; *Census of the State of Michigan, 1894: Agriculture, Manufactories, Mines and Fisheries* 2: pp. 2–507.

substantial increases for these years with the most spectacular
rates of growth concentrated between 1854 and 1874. In
this twenty-year period, growth in the production of staple
crops compared favorably with the four-fold increase in population. Corn increased three and one-half times, while
wheat, other grains, and hay rose almost eight-fold, five-fold,
and nineteen-fold respectively. Increases for the next twenty
years failed to match those for the earlier period. Corn production expanded less than 2 per cent, wheat increased just
slightly under 40 per cent, other grains rose 67 per cent,
and the output of hay inceased slightly over 70 per cent.
None of these figures equaled the 168 per cent rise in population for the same period.

Livestock and dairy production followed a comparable pattern of development. The number of cattle increased five-
fold by 1874 and then rose only 36 per cent in the next
twenty years. Likewise, the number of sheep increased from
zero in 1854 to 952 by 1874 and then rose by less than 20
per cent in the following two decades. Swine provided the
only exception to these patterns. Between 1854 and 1874,
the number of swine declined slightly and then almost tripled
in the next two decades. Rapid growth rates for dairy production were followed by much slower rates of expansion.
The number of milch cows quadrupled by 1874 and then
increased only 29 per cent in the next twenty years. Similarly
butter production showed a sevenfold rise during the early
period and only a 60 per cent increase in the latter period.

Although rapid, the growth and development of the Holland community varied over time. Population growth, for
example, accelerated much more rapidly before 1870 than
afterwards while more concentrated population centers
emerged after 1870. In spite of this growth, however, the
population as indicated by the labor force remained over-
whelmingly of Dutch origin. The community's economic development varied not only over time but also according to
the sector of the economy. Agricultural output rose sharply
until the early 1870's then tapered off. Recording large
growth rates throughout the entire period, the industrial sector, perhaps because of transportation improvements which
by 1870 had tied the settlement to both regional and national
markets, experienced its fastest per capita growth after 1870

which more than offset decline in agriculture at this time. Cumulatively, these economic changes resulted in the community's gradual transition from a rural based economy to one increasingly dependent on light industry.

III.

These economic developments produced major alterations in the occupational structure of the community. The proportion of people directly involved in agriculture as either farm operators or rural workers declined (see table 7). In 1850 the federal census placed 45.9 per cent in farm occupations. This appears to be a very low estimate of the actual number involved since the vast majority of the 35.6 per cent of the labor force classified as laborers in 1850 more than likely worked in agriculture. At this time the primitive state of the community's industry limited employment possiblities for this unskilled labor group to agriculture where they performed such work as clearing land and/or tilling the soil for other farmers. Assuming that most of those enumerated as laborers in 1850 were actualy involved in some type of agricultural pursuit, changes in the community's occupational structure indicate a marked trend away from agricultural employment. The proportion of the labor force involved in farming declined from slightly over 70 per cent in 1860 to slightly more than 50 per cent in both 1870 and 1880.

In addition to the relative decreases, the composition of the agricultural labor force underwent major changes during these years. With the clearing of land, the proportion of farm operators and the percentage of those possessing more valuable farms increased dramatically. Between 1850 and 1870 the proportion of farm operators steadily increased from 9.0 to 42.9 per cent before declining to 32.6 per cent in 1880. Not only did the number of farm operators generally rise, but also the value of their farms increased. None of the farmers enumerated in 1850 owned farms valued in excess of $5,000. By contrast, 2.9 per cent of the labor force fell into this classification in 1880. Similarly that segment composed of farm operators with farms valued in the $1,001 to $5,000 range steadily increased attaining a high of 27.6 per cent of the labor force in 1870 before declining to 21.6 per cent in 1880. The proportion of farmers with farms valued at

TABLE 7
CHANGING OCCUPATIONAL STRUCTURE OF THE HOLLAND COMMUNITY, 1850–1894

Occupation	1850 No.	1850 %	1860 No.	1860 %	1870 No.	1870 %	1880 No.	1880 %	1894[a] No.	1894[a] %
White-collar Workers	23	4.2	67	6.5	204	13.5	316	14.9	358	17.9
Professional	10	1.8	20	1.9	36	2.4	64	3.0	70	3.5
Big Businessmen[b]	1	0.2	7	0.7	34	2.2	44	2.1	...	...
Small Businessmen[c]	11	2.0	29	2.8	111	7.3	150	7.1	136	6.8
Clerical & Sales	1	0.2	11	1.1	23	1.5	58	2.7	152	7.6
Blue-collar Workers	281	50.0	234	22.7	511	33.8	678	32.0	1,610	80.4
Skilled Workers	80	14.2	125	12.1	208	13.7	275	13.0	432	21.6
Semiskilled Workers	1	0.2	36	3.5	99	6.5	288	13.6	979	48.9
Unskilled Workers	200	35.6	73	7.1	204	13.5	115	5.4	199	9.9
Farm Operators	50	8.8	321	31.1	649	42.9	690	32.6	...	...
Farmers (over $5,000)	0	0.0	0	0.0	26	1.7	61	2.9	...	...
Farmers ($1,001–$5,000)	8	1.4	115	11.2	416	27.5	462	21.8	...	...
Farmers ($501–$1,000)	8	1.4	133	12.9	156	10.3	129	6.1	...	...
Farmers (under $500)	34	6.0	73	7.1	51	3.4	38	1.8	...	...
Rural Workers	208	37.1	409	39.6	149	9.8	432	20.4	34	1.7
Gardeners	2	0.4	8	0.8	7	0.5	5	0.2	1	0.0
Tenants & Sharecroppers[d]	0	0.0	0	0.0	0	0.0	19	0.9		0.0
Farmers Without Farms	195	34.7	277	26.9	89	5.9	172	8.1	15	0.7
Farm Laborers	11	2.0	124	12.0	53	3.5	236	11.2	18	0.9
Total	562	100.1	1,031	99.9	1,513	100.0	2,116	99.9	2,002	100.0

[a] Indicates data for only the city of Holland. The manuscripts of the state census are not available for Holland Township or Zeeland.

[b] This category includes businessmen listed in the industrial census as being the owner or partner in a concern with a capitalization in excess of $1,000.

[c] This category includes all those listed in the general census as public officials, merchants, proprietors and managers, and who are not listed in the industrial census as being the owner or partner in a concern with a capitalization of $1,000 or more.

[d] Tenants and sharecroppers were first designated as such in the 1880 census.

Source: Manuscripts of the Seventh Census of the United States, 1850: Population of the United States; Manuscripts of the Eighth Census of the United States, 1860: Population of the United States; Manuscripts of the Ninth Census of the United States, 1870: Population of the United States; Manuscripts of the Tenth Census of the United States, 1880: Population of the United States; (Microfilmed), Michigan State Library; Manuscripts of the Census of the State of Michigan, 1894, Michigan State Archives.

$1,000 or less, after increasing from 7.4 to 20.0 per cent between 1850 and 1860, dropped to 7. per cent by 1880.

In contrast to farm operators, the proportion of rural workers within the labor force, although with some variation among specific occupations in this category, showed an overall decline. After a modest rise from 37.1 to 39.6 per cent between 1850 and 1860, the proportion of rural workers fell precipitously to 9.8 per cent in 1870 before rising to 20.4 per cent in 1880. Among these occupations, gardeners, tenant farmers, and sharecroppers never represented more than 1 per cent of the labor force in the years under consideration. On the other hand, the proportion of farm laborers fluctuated widely. While the 1850 census grossly underestimates the number of farm laborers, their proportion for the remaining censuses fell from 12.0 per cent in 1860 to 3.5 per cent in 1870 before increasing to 11.2 per cent in 1880.

The last remaining occupational group "farmers without farms," which constituted a steadily decreasing proportion of the population, requires further explanation. The term "farmers without farms" refers to those individuals listed as farmers in the general census of population, but who were not enumerated in the census of agriculture. Owing to the large number of them, their omission from the census of agriculture appears to be more than just an oversight on the part of the census taker. Historians dealing with this phenomenon have advanced a number of theories to explain who these people were. Gates in his essay "Frontier Estate Builders and Farm Laborers" considers them to be farm tenants. In his examination of the Iowa and Illinois prairies, Bogue also suggests that many of them were tenants, particularly those listed in the general census without property. On the other hand, Throne argues that many were farm laborers residing in households separate from their place of employment. Curti in his Trempealeau County study offers a third alternative. Conceiving of them as an entity unto themselves, Curti sees them as simultaneously being farmers and farm laborers, farmers in the sense that they owned land, but land which had not yet been cleared. While in the process of clearing their own land, these men worked for other farmers in order to earn a living and purchase needed equipment and livestock. This view best fits the data available for the Holland community. As in Trempealeau County, most of the "farmers without farms" were listed as owning property but omitted from the agricultural census. In addition, this group was more numerous during the early years of the settlement when much of the land remained uncleared than in later years when most of the land had been cleared. In both 1850 and 1860, these farmers comprised more than one-fourth of the labor force. By contrast, only 5.9 and 8.1 per cent respectively of the labor force in 1870 and 1880 fell into this category. That in 1880 tenants and sharecroppers represented less than 1 per cent of the labor force indicates that not only was tenancy not common but also "farmers without farms" were not ten-ants but occupied some other type of a middle position be-tween farm laborers on the one hand and farm operators on the other in the Holland community.[26]

Like the agricultural labor force, the non-farm work force also underwent significant changes. Not only did its size in-crease both relatively and absolutely, but also its composition was transformed. Between 1850 and 1880 the proportion of white-collar positions rose over threefold to 14.9 per cent of the labor force. Within this group the business and propri-etor groups registered the greatest absolute increase jumping from 1.9 per cent of the labor force in 1850 to 7.1 per cent in 1880. At the same time the percentage of professionals expanded from 1.8 to 3.5 per cent while the clerical and sales group displayed the largest relative increase in rising from 0.2 to 2.7 per cent of the labor force.

With the exception of 1850 when a large number of agricul-tural workers were classified as unskilled laborers, data from the federal censuses also indicate that the urban blue-collar workers' share of the work force rose. Between 1860 and 1870 the percentage of the labor force fallng into this cate-gory increased from 22.7 to 33.8 per cent before declining only slightly in 1880. Within this group, the largest gains occurred among the semi-skilled workers whose share of the labor force rose from practically nothing in 1850 to 13.6 per cent in 1880. This category, consisting primarily of fac-tory operatives, indicates the effects of industrialization on

---

[26] Gates, 1957: pp. 145–147; Bogue, 1963: pp. 63–64; Throne, 1959: p. 308; Curti, 1959: pp. 59–60.

the community's occupational structure. By contrast, the proportion of skilled workers in the community remained fairly constant throughout this period never varying by more than 2 per cent in any census between 1850 and 1880. Unlike the skilled workers, the proportion of unskilled workers fluctuated erratically. Even if the data from the 1850 census are excluded because of the inclusion of a number of farm laborers in the unskilled workers category, the proportion of unskilled workers in the labor force rose from 7.2 per cent in 1860 to 13.4 per cent the following decade before falling to 5.4 per cent in 1880.

These changes in the occupational structure reflect the more rapid development of the industrial sector of the economy. The number of factory operatives, as indicated by the data on semi-skilled workers, increased substantially. In addition, the beginnings of a bureaucratic structure commonly associated with industrialism manifested itself in the proportion of the labor force holding white-collar positions especially at the sales and clerical level. Data gathered from the state census of 1894 for the city of Holland further illustrate this trend. By this date almost one-fifth of the city's labor force held white-collar positions with 7.6 per cent falling into the clerical and sales category while semi-skilled workers comprised almost half of the city's working force.

Thus, the economic development of the Holland community precipitated a transformation of its labor force. Not only did the size of the labor force increase with the expansion of the economy, but also a redistribution within the occupational structure took place. Between 1850 and 1880 the proportion of the labor force involved in agriculture steadily decreased while the proportion holding urban occupations steadily increased thus reflecting the increasing importance of the factory in the community's economic life.

III. Migration, Mobility, and the Transformation of the Occupational Structure of the Holland Community*

I.

THE GROWTH and increasing industrialization of the Holland community precipitated not only an expansion of the labor force but also a redistribution within the occupational structure. Alterations in the size and composition of a community's labor force may be viewed as the function of three factors—migration, natural or vital processes, and vertical mobility. Two of these processes serve to alter the size of the labor force, net-migration—the differential between in- and out-migration—and net natural processes, that is, the balance between those entering the labor force for the first time as a result of achieving adulthood and those leaving through either death or retirement. While these processes account for changes in the size of the labor force, they also provide channels through which a community can fulfill its fluctuating occupational needs and thus transform its occupational structure. A third factor, net occupational mobility, although not affecting the size of the labor force, offers another avenue by which a community can meet its varying occupational needs and consequently is an additional source of change in the composition of the labor force. The following analysis will evaluate both the effects of these factors on both the size and the composition of the community's labor force and the relationship between migration and occupational mobility in Holland.

---

* A revised version of this chapter co-authored with Carolyn Tyirin Kirk appeared in the Winter, 1974, issue of the *Journal of Social History*.

By tracing the careers of all these individuals through the federal censuses, it is possible to determine rates of net occupational mobility, net natural processes, and in-, out-, and net-migration. The rate of net occupational mobility for each occupational classification is obtained by subtracting the number of occupationally mobile out of that category from the number of occupationally mobile into that category and dividing the result by the total number in that category at the end of the decade.

Rates of net natural processes for this study are determined by the following procedures.[1] In addition to tracing the careers of all adult males, the father's name, where applicable, has also been recorded which makes it possible to determine the number of new entrants into the labor force as a result of achieving adulthood. A new entrant then is one whose father was listed in a census preceding one in which the son is listed as having an occupation. Data on death rates are based on estimates derived from the manuscripts of the federal census reporting social statistics. These data provide a listing of all who die during the census year. Thus, the deaths in the labor force have been estimated for a given decade by dividing the number of deaths reported in both the census immediately preceding that decade and the census concluding that decade by two. The resulting figure multiplied by ten gives an estimate of the number who died in a decade. Furthermore, for part of the analysis the total estimated number of deaths has been apportioned among the occupations within the labor force using the occupational distribution existing at the beginning of the decade. Net natural processes has been calculated by subtracting the estimated number of deaths and those listed as retired for the first time from the total number of new entrants into the labor force. This procedure may overestimate the number of deaths since it includes newcomers who died in the decade of their in-migration. Furthermore, it assumes that the census years are representative of other years in a given decade. That no other data on deaths exist necessitates such a procedure; evidence from the community found in local histories, mem-

---

[1] Net natural processes may appear to be a misnomer for the process described. In this context, however, it refers specifically to "births" and "deaths" within the labor force and not to births and deaths within the larger Holland community.

oirs, and newspapers, moreover, does not indicate that the years between censuses exhibited extremely high or low death rates.

Number of out-migrants has been determined by subtracting the estimated number of deaths from the number appearing at the beginning of a decade but not present at the end of the decade. Likewise, subtracting the number of new entrants from the number not present at the beginning of a decade but enumerated in the following census indicates the number of in-migrants. Net-migration represents the differential between in- and out-migration. For part of the analysis similar calculations have been made for each occupational group in the Holland community. The figures resulting from these procedures serve as the basis for calculating various rates of migration.

II.

The thirty-year period between 1850 and 1880 witnessed a spectacular expansion of the Holland community's labor force as the number of employed males increased almost four-fold, jumping from 562 to 2,116 (see table 8). A net gain of this magnitude, moreover, involved a turnover of more than 4,000 people based on decennial census data.[2] Accounting for almost 85 per cent of the increase, net-migration was the most important source of increase in the size of the labor force. By contrast, net natural forces represented only 15 per cent of the expansion in the labor supply.

Although migration by far supplied the largest proportion of the gain in the number of employed males in this thirty-year period, its influence waned after 1870. In the two decades prior to this date, combined gains through net-migration not only equaled total increments in the labor force but also offset losses resulting from the deficit through net natural processes. In the 1850's net gains from migration numbered 443 while similar increases from natural forces totaled only 26, and the following decade saw gains through net-migration exceed the expansion of the labor force by 37.

With increases through net natural processes exercising

---

[2] No doubt if this measurement were calculated on an annual basis, the turnover rate would have been much higher.

TABLE 8

Sources of Increase in the Labor Force of the Holland Community, 1850–1880

Decade	In-Migration	Out-Migration	Net-Migration	New Adults	Deaths	Retirement	Net Natural Processes	Total	Net-Migration Per Cent of Increase	Net Natural Processes Per Cent of Increase
1850–60	590	147	443	104	75	3	26	469	94.5	5.5
1860–70	814	295	519	77	105	9	−37	482	107.7	−7.7
1870–80	823	466	357	492	210	36	246	603	59.2	40.8
Total	2,227	908	1,319	673	390	48	235	1,554	84.9	15.1

a more positive role in the growth of the labor force than before, the 1870's marked a turning point in the migration history of the community. The differential between new adults entering the labor force and those leaving through either death or retirement constituted 246 persons or about 40 per cent of the total expansion of the labor force. By contrast, increases emanating from migration, although continuing to be the largest source of change, were relatively less important than earlier. In this decade, expansion due to net-migration decreased in absolute terms from 519 the previous decade to 357 and in relative terms from over 100 per cent to just under 60 per cent of the total increase.

III.

Although net-migration rather than net natural processes most fully explains gains in the size of the labor force, an analysis of the changing composition of the occupational structure must also consider internal changes resulting from occupational movement. That is, one may have a situation where net-migration greatly enlarges the size of the labor force but where new occupational needs are met by members of the existing community as a result of either occupational mobility or new adults entering the labor force.

From a different perspective, every community has its occupational needs. The degree to which newly created occupational openings are not filled through net occupational mobility and net natural processes represents the failure of a community to meet its occupational needs internally and is manifested in changes resulting from net-migration. That is, to the extent that a community cannot satisfy its own demands, it must meet them by attracting a sufficient number of migrants who possess the needed occupational skills. Likewise, those members of the labor force who fail to adjust to the changes in the economy may have to leave the community and go elsewhere in search of employment.

The role of these processes in altering the occupational structure of the Holland community varied both from decade to decade and among occupational groups. In spite of these fluctuations, net-migration was the most dynamic element in altering the composition of the labor force. Out of twelve cases, four broad occupational groups over three decades, net-migration accounted for the greatest change in size seven times between 1850 and 1880 (see table 9). Net occupational mobility, by contrast, was the major source of change in two occupational groups in the 1850's and one in the 1860's, and net natural processes was the most dynamic force in two groups in the 1870's.

More specifically, within the urban labor force, net-migration played a more important role than the other two processes in suppying increases to blue-collar positions. In every decade it provided the main source of growth to this category representing at least 20 per cent of this group. In contrast, net occupational mobility made negative contributions to the blue-collar group in every decade and only in the 1870's did net natural processes yield an increase.

Gains among white-collar workers due to net-migration were relatively less important. Although increases to the white-collar labor force from net-migration in the first two decades under consideration exceeded those provided by the other two sources of change, the magnitude of these differences failed to equal similar differentials in the blue-collar category in all three decades. Such increases, representing

TABLE 9

COMPONENTS OF CHANGE IN THE LABOR FORCE OF THE HOLLAND COMMUNITY BASED ON BROAD OCCUPATIONAL CATEGORIES BY DECADES, 1850–1880[a]

Occupation	Net-Migration		Net Occupational Mobility		Net Natural Processes	
	No.	%	No.	%	No.	%
1850–1860[b]						
White-collar	31	52.2	13	19.4	0	0.0
Blue-collar	82	35.0	−104	−44.4	−25	−10.7
Farm Operators	117	36.4	150	46.7	4	1.2
Rural Workers	213	52.1	−59	−14.4	47	11.5
1860–1870						
White-collar	91	44.6	40	19.6	6	2.9
Blue-collar	300	58.7	−17	−3.3	−6	−1.2
Farm Operators	202	31.1	141	21.7	−15	−2.3
Rural Workers	−74	−49.7	−164	−110.1	−22	−14.8
1870–1880						
White-collar	43	13.6	25	7.9	44	13.9
Blue-collar	138	20.4	−36	−5.3	65	9.6
Farm Operators	91	13.2	16	2.3	−66	−9.6
Rural Workers	85	19.7	−5	−1.2	203	47.0

[a] See Appendix I for a more detailed breakdown by occupation.
[b] All percentages based on the size of the labor force at the end of each decade.

over half of the white-collar workers in 1860, fell to almost
13 per cent by 1880. On the other hand, growth from the
two internal processes, net occupational mobility and net
natural processes, became increasingly important and by the
1870's their combined contribution provided the major
source of expansion within the white-collar group. These
developments in the white-collar group, furthermore, were
a result not only of the decrease in net-migration but also
of an increase due to net natural processes from 0.0 to 13.9
per cent between 1860 and 1880, which more than offset
the decline in the net occupational mobility rate from close
to 20 per cent in the 1850's and 1860's to just under 8 per
cent in the 1870's. Thus, net-migration, insofar as it fulfilled
the changing occupational needs of the non-agricultural labor
force, tended to be relatively more important in the least
economically desirable positions.

Similar to the pattern found in the urban labor force, net-
migration tended to supply a disproportionately larger increase or smaller decrease to the economically less prestigious agricultural category. That is, the difference between
net-migration and the two internal processes combined was
more positive for the rural-workers group than for the farm-
operator category except for the 1870's, when net natural
processes became the largest contributor to change in the
rural-workers category. Subtracting the combined contribution of the internal processes from that of net-migration
for the farm-operators group yields differences of −11.5,
12.7, and 19.5 per cent for the 1850's, 1860's, and 1870's
respectively. Similar calculations for the rural-workers category provide figures of 55.0, 75.2, and −26.1 per cent for
the same three decades.

Despite this similarity in the role of net-migration, changes
in the composition of the agricultural labor force deviated
in a number of respects from the patterns delineated in the
examination of urban occupations. As in white-collar positions, the proportion of farm operators due to either net-
migration or net occupational mobility declined. In contrast
to the white-collar positions, net occupational mobility
showed the steepest decline, and net natural processes declined rather than increased.

Even though net-migration made a more positive contribution to the rural-workers group than did the two internal

processes combined during the first two decades, an analysis of all three components taken separately reveals a somewhat different pattern. In the 1850's the three components of change played the same relative role in the rural-workers category that they had in the blue-collar category throughout the entire period. In addition, net occupational mobility had the greatest negative effect on the rural-workers group in every decade. In contrast to the blue-collar category, however, after 1860 net natural processes was the most positive factor and net-migration followed a middle path between the other two forces in altering the composition of the rural-workers category.

The different patterns of change exhibited by the agricultural labor force could have been due to its decline in relative terms. Within the farm-operators category, all three components came to play increasingly diminishing roles in increasing the size of this group. This indicates that entrance into the farm-operators category was becoming more restrictive over time to new adults, newcomers, and members of other occupational groups. Such a trend corresponds, in the 1870's, to a decrease in the proportion of farm operators in the labor force although the wealthiest sub-category continued to increase proportionately. This suggests that perhaps it became less feasible to subsist as a small farm operator. It also points to the possibility that land, particularly good farm land, became increasingly scarce as a result of population growth and thus made it more difficult for those outside of the farm operator category to gain entrance into that group. Such explanations may also account for the patterns of change among rural workers where net occupational mobility made the greatest negative or the least positive (1870's) contribution, and net natural processes increasingly made the most positive contribution. Such trends reflect the fact that a large proportion of rural workers were farmers' sons who would ultimately take over all or part of the family farm.[3]

---

[3] My data indicate that farm operators' sons comprised 11.2, 11.4, and 51.1 per cent of the rural workers in 1860, 1870, and 1880 respectively. Such a trend may reflect the fact that, as small farmers were declining (presumably for economic reasons) and the land-man ratio was decreasing, farmers were unable to pass on part of their farms to their sons until a later time. Greven, Jr., 1970: passim., has offered a similar explanation for the effects of a decreasing land-man ratio in that town.

IV.

The ease with which changes in the size and composition of the labor force resulting from migration can be sketched obscures the complexity of this process. That the net-gain of 1,319 working males between 1850 and 1880 involved the movement of over 3,000 people, a figure one and one-half times the size of the labor force in 1880, indicates that migration is an extremely complex phenomenon having a greater impact on a community than is expressed by its net contribution to the growth of the labor force. Thus a clearer understanding of the relationship between migration and occupational mobility requires a detailed examination of both in- and out-migration by occupational group. In the following analysis, percentage rates of in- and net-migration will be based on the size of the labor force in the last year of the decade and out-migration rates will be based on the size of the labor force at the beginning of the decade.

During the years under consideration rates of out-migration remained relatively constant, rising only about 2 per cent per decade from 26 to 31 per cent. By contrast, rates of in-migration varied more and decreased steadily from 57 to 39 per cent between 1850 and 1880 (see table 10). Given the constancy of out-migration rates, this also means that net-migration varied widely and declined. Thus, during these years Holland experienced substantial population turnover; in every decade between one-fourth and one-third of the male adult labor force departed and an even larger number of newcomers entered the labor force.

More important for an understanding of the relationship between migration and the occupational structure is the fact that these gross changes in the in- and out-migration rates camouflage wide variations among occupational groups. That is, not only did the Holland community experience substantial population turnover, but also patterns of in- and out-migration tended to be related to occupational class. In general both rates of in- and out-migration were highest in the less economically remunerative positions.

With the exception of the 1850's, the highest rates of out-migration occurred at the bottom of the occupational structure. In this first decade, little variation existed among occu-

TABLE 10

MIGRATION RATES FOR THE HOLLAND COMMUNITY BASED ON BROAD OCCUPATIONAL
CATEGORIES BY DECADE, 1850–1880[a]

Occupation	In-Migration		Out-Migration		Net-Migration	
	No.	%	No.	%	No.	%
1850–1860	590	57.2	147	26.2	443	43.0
White-collar	40	59.7	9	39.1	31	49.2
Blue-collar	166	70.9	84	29.1	82	35.0
Farm Operators	128	39.9	11	22.0	117	36.4
Rural Workers	256	62.6	43	20.7	213	52.1
1860–1870	814	53.8	295	28.7	519	34.3
White-collar	109	53.4	18	26.9	91	44.6
Blue-collar	381	74.6	81	34.6	300	58.7
Farm Operators	241	37.1	39	12.1	202	31.1
Rural Workers	83	55.7	157	38.4	−74	−49.7
1870–1880	823	38.9	466	30.8	357	16.9
White-collar	113	35.8	70	34.3	43	13.6
Blue-collar	366	54.0	228	44.6	138	20.4
Farm Operators	183	26.5	92	14.2	91	13.2
Rural Workers	161	37.3	76	51.0	85	19.7

[a]See Appendix II for a more detailed breakdown by occupation.

pational groups. Excluding the sales and clerical group and gardeners, who numbered three people in 1850, only the out-migration rate of 60 per cent for professionals deviated by more than 8 per cent from the community average of 25 per cent.

In contrast to the 1850's, rates of departure in the two succeeding decades corresponded closely to occupational levels. Out-migration rates for rural workers in both decades were more than three times greater than those for farm operators. Moreover, none of the rates for specific occupations within the farm-operators category approached those for any occupational group within the rural-workers classification. A similar pattern prevailed for non-agricultural occupational groups. Although in the first decade white-collar rates of departure exceeded by 10 per cent those for blue-collar workers, the following two decades found the pattern reversed with blue-collar rates being 7 and 10 per cent higher respectively.

While patterns of departure were similar for both the agri-

cultural and urban labor forces, the differential in out-migration rates between farm operators and rural workers far exceeded the differential between white- and blue-collar
workers. One explanation for these developments might be
that as the community's occupational needs changed as a
result of the economy's greater reliance on light industry
rather than agriculture there was a greater scarcity of economic resources for those at the bottom of the agricultural
labor force than for blue-collar workers. That is, between
1860 and 1870 the absolute number of rural workers declined. The increase in the absolute number in the 1870's,
furthermore, coincided both with a decrease in small yeoman
farmers and an increase in large farm operators which suggests that small farms were becoming less feasible while positions working for large farm operators with little opportunity
for advancement into the farm-operator category were becoming more numerous. That out-migration rates were highest among rural workers in both the 1860's and 1870's further
supports this view.

Even more clearly than patterns of out-migration, rates
of in-migration tended to be highest in positions at the bottom of the occupational ladder. Within the agricultural labor
force, migration into the rural-workers category surpassed
that for the farm-operators category by at least 10 per cent
in all three decades. Perhaps more indicative of this pattern
is the fact that in only one decade, the 1870's, did in-migration account for more than 10 per cent of the wealthiest
farm operator group. On the other hand, in only one decade
did in-migration equal less than 50 per cent of the farm-
laborer group. A similar pattern existed among non-agricultural occupations; in every decade, rates of in-migration into
blue-collar occupations exceeded by at least 10 per cent those
into white-collar groups. Furthermore, higher rates of in-migration prevailed for white-collar workers than for farm operators and for blue-collar workers than for rural workers. In
addition, in-migration rates for white-collar workers ranged
within 3 per cent of the rates for rural workers over the
three decades.

Such findings concerning in-migration further support our
suggested explanation for higher out-migration rates for agricultural workers. Though there was absolute growth throughout the period within all four broad occupational groups,

farm-operator positions were declining proportionately which resulted in less potential security or advancement within the agricultural labor force. This, in turn, induced greater out-migration and less in-migration within that sector than within the non-agricultural sector. Such an explanation appears to contradict the work of both Morrison and Lowry who argue that in-migration rates correspond to local economic conditions while out-migration rates do not. Their studies, however, examine the overall in- and out-migration rates for a community and not groups within the community. The Holland data indicate, however, that the two rates vary widely among occupational categories and that the best possible explanation at this time appears to be that out-migration rates as well as in-migration rates reflect changes in the local economy and corresponding changes in the structure of the work force.[4]

Although few detailed community studies of in- and out-migration exist, there are a number of investigations of decennial rates of persistence denoting what proportion of male adults present at the beginning of a decade remain throughout the ten-year period. In order to facilitate comparisons with these studies, which did not distinguish between internal losses through death and external losses through migration, the persistence rates were computed for Holland by adding the estimated number of deaths and out-migrations together and then subtracting the result from the total labor force population at the beginning of the decade.

The persistence rates in Holland for the three decades between 1850 and 1880 of 61, 61, and 55 per cent respectively are comparable to other findings and, if anything, tend toward the high side. More specifically, comparisons with Stephan Thernstrom's compilation of persistence rates for selected urban areas between 1800 and 1958 indicates that the Holland community did not differ significantly from these communities. In more than three-quarters (24 of 31) of the cases he listed, persistence rates were between 40 and 60 per cent. It should be further noted that Thernstrom found that persistence rates did not vary over time, among types of cities or among cities experiencing different growth rates.[5]

---

[4] Morrison, 1970: p. 15 and Lowry, 1966: *passim.*

[5] Thernstrom, 1970: *passim.*

These patterns of persistence held not only for most cities in the last century and two-thirds but also for rural communities. In only 8 of the 26 communities included in the compilation did persistence rates fall outside of the 40 to 60 per cent range; furthermore, communities in the early years of settlement accounted for 7 of the 8 deviant cases. In these settlements no more than a third of the adult males remained more than a decade. After this initial period of extreme fluidity, however, rural persistence rates approached the general level of those in cities.[6]

The magnitude of the difference between the persistence rates for the Holland community during its first two decades and these other new rural settlements suggests a more complex explanation than mere chance. One possible explanation is that rapidly growing areas would be more likely to keep their existing population. A comparison of population growth rates between Holland and three other new settlements for which data are readily available from the U.S. Census does not indicate that this is a valid explanation. Both Wapello County, Iowa, and selected townships in eastern Kansas had growth rates about 15 per cent below Holland's 84 per cent. The population of Trempealeau County, however, increased over four-fold in its first decade. Thus high persistence does not appear to be a correlate of rapid population growth in new settlements.[7]

A second possible explanation for the high persistence rates in the Holland community is that opportunity for advancement was greater there than in any of these other settlements. That is, it might be assumed that a community offering high levels of occupational mobility would be better able to retain its population than one that did not. Unfortunately data on occupational mobility exist only for Trempealeau County and Holland, thus making any conclusions regarding this relationship only suggestive. The existing data do indi-

---

[6] *Ibid.,* pp. 225–227.

[7] Data for Iowa are for employed males from Throne, 1959: pp. 305–330; data for Trempealeau County are for employed males from Curti, 1959: *passim.;* eastern Kansas data are for farm operators in sample townships from Malin, 1935: pp. 339–372. Population figures for the remaining four areas; East-central Kansas, 1860–1870; Roseburg, Oregon, 1870–1880; Grant County, Wisconsin, 1885–1895; and West Kansas, 1895–1905 were not available in the federal census of population.

cate that greater opportunity existed in Holland than in Trempealeau County. During the first decade of their existence, rates of total and upward occupational mobility were 64 and 33 per cent respectively in the former and 43 and 21 per cent in the latter settlement. Such findings, although tentative at best, suggest that social scientists should look more fully at the relationship between vertical and geographic mobility in the nineteenth century.[8]

Another possible explanation that seems likely is based on cultural and organizational factors. The founders of the Holland area sought to establish a homogeneous Christian community. As a result, it may be that the advance planning of the community along with its ethnic homogeneity and religious commitment offered an element of population stability in the early years that was not existent in these other settlements. That the persistence rate for the Dutch-born population in the 1870's was almost double that of the non-Dutch native born population (57 to 31 per cent) further underscores the importance of these factors in explaining the settlement's high persistence rates during its early years. Similarly, those born in the United States of Dutch parentage had almost as high a persistence rate (56 per cent) as the Dutch-born even though most were under thirty—an age group generally found to be the most geographically mobile. It should be noted, however, that in cities where ethnically homogeneous communities formed without prior planning or commitment, this type of stability did not exist.[9]

Although any explanation at this point must remain tentative, the data indicate that the population growth rate in new settlements is not a determinant of persistence. On the other hand, occupational mobility and ethnic homogeneity do seem to be related to persistence in new settlements. Based on the internal evidence from Holland on the differing persistence rates of the Dutch and the non-Dutch, an explana-

---

[8] Occupational mobility for purposes of this examination was defined as movement from one of four broad occupational groups (urban white-collar, urban blue-collar, farm-operator, rural-worker) to another. Upward occupational mobility included only movement from a blue-collar to a white-collar position and mobility from the rural-workers to the farm-operators category. For a further analysis of mobility in Trempealeau County, see Curti, 1959: pp. 140–258. Chapters IV and V will offer a further analysis of occupational mobility in the Holland community.

[9] Thernstrom, 1970: p. 232.

tion based on cultural and organizational factors in new communities is favored. But this explanation must remain only suggestive until further studies are undertaken which explicitly explore the degree of ethnic and religious homogeneity and the organizational nature of settlements at their foundings. While favoring this argument, neither the possibility of a relationship between opportunity and persistence nor an explanation based on a combination of both organizational factors and opportunity is ruled out. In order to test the relationship between occupational mobility and persistence in new settlements, moreover, attention should focus on what skills are being favored in occupational mobility and the extent to which the existing population possesses those skills or can acquire them readily.

It is impossible, furthermore, to understand fully the relationship between occupational mobility and persistence and the effect of cultural and organizational factors on it unless out-migration is separated from deaths. That is, studies of persistence assume implicitly that the age structure and the death rate remain constant both within all ethnic segments of a community and between communities. This leads to a further assumption that the out-migration rate encompasses approximately the same proportion of the persistence rate's residual, i.e., out-migration equals persistence rate minus a constant. Thus studies more sensitive to the death rate will facilitate more meaningful comparisons of differing rates of persistence.

More importantly for an understanding of the relationship between migration and labor-force composition is the fact that the type of men who were most transient in Holland were also the most transient in other nineteenth-century American communities. In the Holland settlement, in- and out-migration rates were higher for blue- than white-collar workers and for rural workers than farm operators. Similarly Thernstrom found that in the ten available tabulations for selected nineteenth- and early twentieth-century cities blue-collar workers had lower rates of persistence than white-collar employees.[10] In addition, a recalculation of the available data pertaining to persistence in three rural communities indicates

[10] *Ibid.*, pp. 228–232.

that similar patterns of turnover existed in these areas (see table 11). In every case persistence rates for farm operators surpassed those of rural workers and those for white-collar workers either exceeded or equaled the rates for blue-collar workers. Thus the selective pattern of out-migration found in Holland occurred in other nineteenth-century communities for which data are available.

Although some studies of persistence exist, no systematic examinations of in-migration are available for the nineteenth century. As a result, it is not possible to determine to what extent the pattern of higher in-migration rates for the less economically prestigious categories in Holland is typical. In the absence of studies to the contrary and given the fact that patterns of out-migration in Holland did not deviate from those of other nineteenth-century communities, there is no reason to suspect that the selective nature of migration into the settlement was unique.

V.

The results of this examination have broader implications for both the nature and study of occupational mobility. If widespread in nineteenth-century America, the tendency of those at the bottom of the occupational ladder to be the most transient as well as the tendency for net-migration to supply disproportionate increases to less prosperous occupations while internal processes disproportionately increased the more prosperous groups implies that the geographically mobile tended to experience less upward vertical movement

TABLE 11

RATES OF PERSISTENCE BY OCCUPATION FOR SELECTED RURAL COMMUNITIES

Name of Settlement	Decade	Farm Operators	Rural Workers	White-Collar	Blue-Collar
Crawford Township	1850–60	24	4	n.a.	n.a.
Crawford Township	1860–70	40	3	n.a.	n.a.
Trempealeau County	1860–70	32	24	33	19
Trempealeau County	1870–80	39	22	25	25
Wapello County	1850–60	46	20	30	18

Source: Bowers, 1950: pp. 8–10; Curti, 1959: pp. 140–258; Throne, 1959: pp. 305–330. Percentages computed by the authors.

than those remaining in a settlement. That is, the nineteenth-century man on the move, unlike his twentieth-century counterpart, cannot be equated with the successful man on the make.[11]

These findings also suggest that studies of occupational mobility in any community are dealing with an unrepresentative sample skewed toward the most occupationally mobile. Thus, any analysis of nineteenth-century mobility based on data drawn from city directories or census manuscripts will inflate upward mobility rates. The degree of inflation, however, is open and will likely remain so for a long time since it is virtually impossible to examine directly the relationship between geographical and occupational mobility because of the difficulty in tracing large numbers of individuals from place to place through the manuscripts of the federal censuses. Such conclusions, however, do not impair the usefulness of community studies of occupational mobility. Only after migration and occupational mobility have been studied in a number of different types of communities can social scientists begin to make more precise inferences about the relationship between migration, persistence, and vertical mobility.

Although the evidence for Holland indicates that migration may not have served as viable an avenue for upward mobility as persistence, it is possible that rates of net-migration and occupational mobility are still related. That is, it might be expected that net-migration would be greatest in those communities having the highest rates of vertical mobility. Data for Holland tend to support this generalization. Both rates of net-migration and upward occupational mobility steadily fell in the three decades between 1850 and 1880 with the former dropping from 43 to 17 per cent and the latter decreasing from 33 to 7 per cent. Likewise gross rates of occupational mobility fell from 64 to 21 per cent.[12]

Because little systematic analysis of the relationship between occupational mobility and net-migration has been conducted, generalizations regarding the relationship of these two variables remain tentative. The only comparable study

---

[11] The most recent and thorough examination of mobility in contemporary America indicates a strong relationship between geographic and upward occupational mobility. Blau and Duncan, 1967: pp. 243–275.

[12] See Chapter IV.

is Sidney Goldstein's examination of Norristown from 1910 to 1950 where he found, in contrast to Holland, that both gross and upward occupational mobility tended to increase as net-migration decreased. From these findings he argues that vertical mobility and migration complement each other in serving to meet the needs of an economy and in bringing about change in the occupational structure.[13]

The contradictory findings between the two studies suggest that the relationship between migration and occupational mobility is more complex than Goldstein suggests and involves other factors affecting both variables. For example, Goldstein's model ignores the impact of net natural processes on altering the size and composition of a labor force. A sudden increase from this process, assuming that the occupational needs of a community remained constant, would certainly bring about a decrease in net-migration and potentially a decrease in occupational mobility. The model assumes also, that occupational mobility is totally structurally induced; however, data indicate that only about half the rate of occupational mobility can be attributed to structural changes in the labor force.[14]

Lastly, implicit in the model is the idea that an increase in the labor-force size will only affect the net-migration rate. However, where both the size of the labor force is increasing and especially where positions at the upper levels of the occupational hierarchy are expanding, it would be expected that both net-migration and occupational mobility would increase.

In conclusion, the findings from this examination suggest that, while certain relationships hold both in the nineteenth and twentieth centuries, others vary implying that the relationships among structure and size of labor force, vertical mobility, migration, persistence, and natural processes may depend on the historical period or period of economic development involved. Moreover, they suggest that some of the relationships generally posited between only two or three of these variables are but special cases of a process involving various factors interacting in a complex manner.

---

[13] Goldstein, 1955: pp. 402–408.

[14] Blau and Duncan, 1967: p. 104, using contemporary survey research data have shown that changes in the occupational structure or more specifically changes in the distribution of occupations among members of their sample accounted for only about 50 per cent of the total observed inter-generational occupational mobility.

IV. Patterns of Intra-generational Occupational Movement in the Holland Community

I.

THE ANALYSIS of social mobility, while a complex problem for sociologists and other students of contemporary society, provides even greater difficulties for historians of the nineteenth century. Most students of social stratification agree in theory at least that a number of complex variables comprise the concepts of class and status. Unfortunately data bearing on many of these variables are simply not available to historians. Illustrative of this is the impossibility of employing the interview technique which students of contemporary society can employ to acquire prestige ratings of individuals by other members of the community.

These limitations necessitate that the historical study of social mobility rely solely on the available objective criteria that make up only a part of the concept of social status. The most commonly employed objective criterion and one available to students of the late nineteenth century is occupational rank. Such an approach to the historical study of mobility does not distinguish historical studies from the overwhelming majority of twentieth-century studies undertaken by sociologists. For while not conceptualizing of occupation as the sole variable in a comprehensive theory of class or status, sociologists have relied upon changes in occupation to infer changes in social status. Such procedures were developed and justified, write Westoff, Bressler, and Sagi, "partly as a concession to methodological difficulties and partly from theoretical considerations supported by empirical evidence." Underlying the latter is the view most recently expressed by Blau and Duncan that occupation more than any other

58

variable has determined or at least has set limits on the other variables in a comprehensive theory of class. Thus students of social mobility, while theoretically acknowledging that many variables shape social status, have frequently based their measurements of social mobility on occupational change.[1]

Using change in occupation as an indicator of change in either social status or any of the components comprising that concept, however, has been seriously questioned by Westoff, Bressler, and Sagi who find that neither inter- nor intra-generational occupational mobility is strongly correlated with any of a large number of hypothesized indices of social mobility. The implication of their study "is that one can not safely infer knowledge of one dimension of mobility from knowledge of another."[2] That their sample includes married couples with two children in their mid- and upper twenties and is based on data collected in a span of only three years means occupational movement probably has been measured before an individual reaches the peak of his career. In addition, the short interval between the first and last observation means that no provisions are made for long-term changes in indices or components of social mobility such as wealth, income, and residence that might not be immediately reflected by a change in occupation. Thus because of these problems, their conclusion regarding the inference of social mobility from occupational movement may be exaggerated.

Nevertheless, the issues they raise indicate the need for social scientists to specify as precisely as possible what is being measured by changes in occupation. This is especially true for historians since they do not have access to data bearing on the other variables commonly used in determining social status and measuring mobility. Recently Stuart Blumin has suggested one way of circumventing these serious obstacles to the historical study of mobility. Arguing that "social mobility may not be the only way of conceptualizing the 'open society,'" he contends that when the self-help literature of the nineteenth century spoke of success, it was invoking a

---

[1] Westoff, Bressler and Sagi, 1960: p. 378 and Blau and Duncan, 1967: p. 120.
[2] Westoff, Bressler, and Sagi, 1960: pp. 383–384.

concept of success that was more economic than social. Economic mobility, moreover, is a far more tangible concept than social mobility in that it offers a more direct concept with which to examine the openness of a society. In addition, it is more easily quantifiable than the less tangible concept of social mobility. "Thus," Blumin reasons, "if we shift our ultimate goal from that of measuring social mobility to that of measuring the closely related but conceptually distinct phenomenon of economic mobility, we may hit upon, if not a necessarily more valid inference, at least a more readily testable one."[3]

Partly because of the lack of adequate data on wealth, Blumin suggests that in ante-bellum Philadelphia it is "virtually impossible to study economic mobility . . . without reverting to the inferential method of occupational mobility."[4] Likewise the data for the Holland community necessitate the use of this inferential method. This is due in part to the lack of probate records and the unorganized nature of the tax records which list the property holdings of individuals in several different places within reports. The failure of these records to provide additional information such as age, wife's name, and children's names also makes it virtually impossible to trace individual careers over time. The most satisfying sources for the Holland community are the manuscript schedules of the federal census which for 1860 and 1870 list each inhabitant's occupation and the value of his real and personal property with the latter designation including both tangible and intangible goods. No doubt these schedules contain a large number of inaccuracies, both honest and dishonest. Nevertheless, because of their inclusiveness and the information contained in them, they are a great aid to the study of economic mobility. Unfortunately the federal census manuscripts of 1880, the state census of 1894, and the data on immigrants from The Netherlands do not contain comparable information on wealth, and the census of 1850 only includes information on real wealth. Therefore, if economic mobility is to be studied for an extended period of time, it will have to be inferred from occupational mobility computed

---

[3] Blumin, 1968: p. 3.
[4] *Ibid.*, p. 4.

by tracing the individual career patterns of members of the community.

Before pursuing such an analysis, the validity of the inference of wealth from occupation will be tested in order to determine the strength of the relationship between occupation and wealth in the Holland community. Relying on data from the manuscripts of the federal census for 1870, the relationship between occupation and total listed wealth was measured. Although data from the census of 1860 could have been used, 1870 data were selected to test the relationship for a number of reasons. One is that data from this year came closest to the median year of the time span of this study. More importantly, by this date the community had matured sufficiently so that, if a relationship existed between wealth and occupation, it would have appeared by then; that is, in the earlier days of the community with vast tracts of unimproved land there was less variation in wealth among members of the community.

In order to analyze this relationship, fifteen occupational groups have been collapsed into four categories, four wealth intervals established, and Eta^2, a measure of intraclass correlation, calculated. This statistic indicates how much of the total variance in wealth can be "explained" by occupation; that is, Eta^2 increases in magnitude as the amount of variation between occupational groups increases relative to the amount of variation within such categories. Thus as the variation in wealth between occupational groups increases Eta^2 will move away from 0 and tend towards 1. Therefore, if Eta^2 equals 1, it indicates that all the variation in wealth occurs between occupational groups and that within any occupational group there is no variation in wealth. Conversely, if there is no variation in wealth between occupational groups, Eta^2 will equal 0.[5]

The results of this analysis suggest that there was a moderately strong relationship between wealth and occupation. When the four by four table is employed, Eta^2 equals .24. This means that occupation in the Holland community accounted for about one-fourth of the variation in wealth. From

---

[5] For a further discussion of analysis of variance see Blalock, Jr., 1960: pp. 242–272.

this, however, it is readily apparent that changes in occupation do not completely explain differences in wealth and gives
some support to the contention of Westoff, *et al.* However,
controlling for age shows that occupation is much more
strongly associated with wealth for older cohorts. Specifically,
establishing five age cohorts of ten years each for those between the ages of twenty-one and seventy reveals that occupation explains over 60 per cent of the variance in wealth for
the three age cohorts over forty. Furthermore, that the
amount of variance explained in the twenty-one to thirty and
thirty-one to forty age groups is only 5.0 and 23.0 per cent
demonstrates that the number of years practicing a particular
occupation affects the amount of wealth each member in that
occupational category has.[6] Thus, although these results suggest that other factors such as the wealth of the individual's
family (including those who may or may not have received
their just inheritance), ambition, size of wife's dowry, number
of children, and frugality may also help to explain wealth,
the high levels of association for the older cohorts support
the contention that improvement in economic condition to
a large extent can be inferred from occupational mobility
in the Holland community.

The strong relationship between occupation and wealth
lends validity to the inference of economic mobility from
occupational mobility. The following chapters, in addition
to including an evaluation of the openness of the Holland
community by employing the concept of economic mobility,
will also contain an examination of the impact of changes
in the occupational structure on mobility patterns. The re-
mainder of this chapter will consist of an analyis of intra-
generational occupational mobility while the following one
will deal with inter-generational movement. Chapter VI will
examine intra-generational wealth mobility using economic
data from the manuscripts of the federal census for 1850,
1860, and 1870 to check further the relationship between
wealth and occupational mobility. In these various analyses,
attention will be focused on trends in mobility and their relationships to structural changes, patterns of movement for

---

[6] Eta^2 for the 21–30, 31–40, 41–50, 51–60, and 61–70 age cohorts are .05, .23,
.63, .63, .60 respectively.

various occupational groups, and a comparison of rates of upward and downward mobility. In the conclusion of this study, these findings will be compared with the results of other mobility studies in order to offer broader generalizations about the openness of nineteenth-century American society.

II.

Two types of occupational classifications will be employed in this analysis. Table 12 presents summary measures of occupational mobility using the same fifteen-point scale as employed in the earlier examination of alterations in the occupational sructure and table 13 collapses those fifteen categories into four—urban white-collar, urban blue-collar, farm operators (those listed in the agricultural census as owners of improved farms), and rural workers (those holding agricultural positions but not listed in the census of agriculture as farm owners). As would be expected and as the data presented in this chapter will confirm, mobility rates are higher for the finer classifications than for the collapsed groups since with the four-point scale only those moving from one broad group to another will be counted among the mobile. In contrast, the fifteen-point scale includes among the occupationally mobile those moving from one occupation to another whether or not it falls in the same broad category. Thus, movement between collapsed occupational groups may be viewed as representing more significant movement than that between the fifteen categories. That is, students of occupational mobility have usually regarded moving from a blue-collar to a white-collar position, for example, as a qualitatively more important change than moving from an unskilled to a semi-skilled position. However, the use of the broad classifications, although measuring mobility generally considered most significant, may also obscure a great deal of movement not involving the crossing of major occupational lines. For example, one could conceive of a society with a great deal of mobility using the finer distinctions and none at all for broad groupings. Thus a man moving from an unskilled to a skilled blue-collar position would not be included among the mobile in the latter type of analysis, although this would no doubt be a meaningful move for the individual involved.

TABLE 12

Summary Measures of Occupational Mobility for the Holland Community Using Fifteen Occupational Groups, 1850–1894

	50–60	50–70	50–80	60–70	60–80	70–80	70–94	80–94
Percentage Mobile								
Observed	75.4	85.3	91.6	70.0	79.6	47.7	48.4	39.5
Minimum Structural Movement	51.6 (39.4)[2]	73.7 (53.8)[2]	83.2 (61.2)[2]	43.9 (35.9)[2]	57.2 (33.8)[2]	11.7 (20.9)[2]	14.7[1] (30.4)[3]	9.8[1] (11.3)[3]
(Observed Minus Minimum) Circulation	23.8	11.6	8.4	26.1	22.4	36.0	33.7	29.7
Cramér V	.379	.344	.270	.433	.364	.478	.397	.422

[1] Data for these years are only for the City of Holland.

[2] Figures in parentheses represent the degree of structure change calculated on the basis of the entire labor force.

[3] For the calculations of structural changes involving 1894 data, some modifications had to be made. Only those employed in urban occupations were included in calculation in order to make the 1894 data comparable to earlier censuses.

TABLE 13
Summary Measures of Occupational Mobility for the Holland Community Using Collapsed Occupational Groups, 1850–1894

	50-60	50-70	50-80	60-70	60-80	70-80	70-94	80-94
Percentage Mobile								
Observed	64.4	76.5	80.7	39.6	47.9	21.2	23.8	19.6
Minimum Structural Movement	48.4 $(27.3)^2$	68.4 $(43.4)^2$	75.7 $(34.1)^2$	28.7 $(29.2)^2$	35.4 $(19.2)^2$	5.1 $(12.0)^2$	4.9^1 $(10.3)^3$	5.6^1 $(13.6)^3$
(Observed Minus Minimum) Circulation	16.0	8.1	5.0	10.9	12.5	16.1	18.9	14.0
Cramér V	.472	.331	.268	.530	.462	.608	.546	.590

[1] Because of the lack of rural occupations in the data for the city of Holland summary measures for these two columns are based on 3 × 3 tables using two urban and one rural occupational classifications.

[2] Figures in parentheses represent the degree of structural change calculated on the basis of the entire labor force.

[3] For the calculations of structural changes involving 1894 data, some modifications had to be made. Only those employed in urban occupations were included in calculation in order to make the 1894 data comparable to earlier censuses.

Thus incorporating both types of occupational categories will
give a fuller understanding of the nature and pattern of occupational mobility than using just one or the other.

Regardless of the type of classification employed, summary
measures of mobility suggest that the occupational structure
of the Holland community became more rigid as time passed
(see tables 12 and 13). Using finer occupational distinctions
indicates that total movement declined from 70 per cent or
more in the two decades before 1870 to less than 50 per
cent for the periods 1870–1880 and 1880–1894. Mobility
rates based on the collapsed occupational categories, furthermore, reveal an even sharper decline, falling from 64.4 per
cent in the first decade to 19.6 per cent for the 1880–1894
time period. Part of this steep decline may be explained by
the fact that many who were listed as laborers in 1850 were
actually rural workers of some type. That slightly more than
60 per cent of the blue-collar workers in 1850 held agricultural positions in 1860 as compared with only about 18 per
cent of the blue-collar workers listed in either 1860 or 1870
and in the respective following census further supports this
contention. However, the fall in gross rates of mobility from
39.6 to 21.2 and from 70.0 to 47.7 per cent between the
1860's and the 1870's using the collapsed and finer occupational scales respectively indicates that the decline in mobility
was due to more than a misclassification of laborers in the
1850 census. Moreover, that the relative decrease in mobility
between the pre- and post-1870 period is far greater using
the four broad categories rather than the finer ones suggests
significant movement across broad occupational lines experienced the greatest decline.

The increasing rigidity of the occupational structure is
demonstrated not only by shrinking rates of occupational
mobility but also by the strength of the relationship between
beginning and ending occupation which rises in each successive time period except for the last one. Cramér V, an overall
measure of association which has an upper limit of unity
indicating a perfect relationship and a lower limit of 0.0 indicating no relationship whatsoever, illustrates the growing
strength of the relationship between beginning and ending
occupation. Using fifteen occupational categories, the correlation between beginning occupation and destination be-

comes increasingly stronger for each succeeding decade between 1850 and 1880, before declining slightly for the years 1880–1894.[7] Similarly, the strength of the relationship between beginning and ending occupation employing four broad occupational categories rises steadily in each decade to 1880 before declining slightly in the 1880–1894 time period. This second set of calculations also reveals much stronger associations between beginning and ending occupation than does the first. Moreover, the differential between the broad and finer occupational groups for each decade and the 1880–1894 time period is at least .093 and becomes progressively larger for later time sequences.

This analysis of gross mobility rates and the relationship between beginning and ending occupation shows that not only did occupational mobility decline and the relationship between beginning and ending occupation grow stronger but also that significant mobility, i.e., movement across the blue-white collar line, the rural worker-farm operator line, and the urban-rural line fell more rapidly than did mobility between finer occupational lines. Thus, it appears that after the initial period of settlement, the social structure of the community became increasingly more rigid, especially after 1870 and particularly in terms of movement from one broad occupational category to another.

The measures in the middle two rows of tables 12 and 13 offer a means of further examining the decline in gross mobility within the community. Minimum structural movement represents the minimum amount of mobility within the mobility matrix necessary to accommodate changes in the occupational structure. That is, such movement expressed as a percentage may be seen as that proportion of gross mobility resulting from changes in the occupational structure. This figure is derived by subtracting the total percentage for each row from the total of each corresponding column of the mobility matrix and then summing either all positive or negative values. Thus, this measure gives both an indica-

---

[7] One explanation for the fact that Cramér V decreased while gross mobility decreased between 1880 and 1894 relates to the 1894 data from the state census. Since it is only for the city of Holland, it disproportionately includes in the sample only those employed in agriculture who moved into urban occupations and thus weakens the relationship between beginning and ending occupation.

tion of what socioeconomic changes contribute to total movement and a theoretical understanding of the mobility process.
The difference beween this figure and observed mobility Jackson and Crockett label circulation or the amount of movement not directly attributable to structural change, i.e., the
mutual exchange of occupations by members of the
community.[8] Computed simply as a residual of minimum
structural movement, circulation has no specific theoretical
foundation. However, it does provide an indication of the
degree to which members of the various occupational groups
exchange places. A second measure of structural change, appearing in parentheses in the second row of tables 12 and
13 is also utilized. Calculated in the same manner as minimum
structural movement but using the entire labor force rather
than just those in the mobility matrix, this indicator probably
provides a better overall index of structural change since it
takes into account alterations in the labor force due to migration and net-natural processes in measuring changes in the
community's occupational structure. However, since both
measurements are useful for gauging the effects of change
on the mobility process, each will be included in the following
analysis.

A closer inspection of these data suggests that mobility
attributable to alterations in the occupational structure declines sharply after 1870, follows the same pattern as gross
mobility rates, and most fully accounts for the decline in
the gross rate of movement. Regardless of the type of occupational classification employed, minimum structural movement, as measured by the mobility matrix, is at least three
times greater in the 1850's and 1860's than in the two time
periods following 1870. Moreover, when the collapsed occu-

---

[8] Jackson and Crockett, 1964: pp. 5–15. In addition to the methods developed
by Jackson and Crockett to break occupational mobility down into its component
parts, Rogoff, 1954: *passim.*, has developed the "full equality" model which is aimed
at eliminating the effects of structural changes from patterns of occupational mobility. I have adopted the Jackson and Crockett model since it includes the effects
of structural change as well as the mutual exchange of occupations on gross mobility.
In addition, there are serious questions regarding the effectiveness of the Rogoff
model in achieving its goals. For a discussion of these methods see Duncan, 1966:
pp. 63–77. Moreover, Blau and Duncan, 1967: p. 97, argue the Rogoff method is
unsuited to making comparisons over time and employ the Jackson and Crockett
model in part of their analysis.

pational categories are employed the decrease in minimum structural movement is greater than when finer occupational distinctions are employed. In the former instance mobility attributable to changes in the occupational structure falls from 44.1 per cent for the first decade to 5.6 per cent for the 1880–1894 time period while in the latter case it drops from 51.6 to 10.1 per cent with the largest decline taking place between the 1860's and 1870's. Basing the measurement of structural movement on the entire labor force rather than only those in the mobility matrix and using collapsed occupational categories again reveal that the steepest decreases occur after 1870 and for the broad occupational schema. Structural changes in the earliest two decades as measured by broad groupings are more than double in the latter two time periods while finer occupational classifications show structural changes before 1870 to be slightly less than double those following 1870.

Furthermore, changes in the amount of structural mobility vary inversely with changes in circulation or the amount of mobility attributable to the mutual exchange of occupations. For the fifteen-point occupational classification, circulation steadily increases in every decade from 1850 to 1880 before declining in the 1880–1894 time period while just the reverse pattern exists for both measures of structural change. With the exception of changes between the decades of the 1850's and 1860's, these trends also prevail for the examination using collapsed occupational categories. Such relationships suggest that the decreased mobility attributable to structural change induced a greater mutual exchange of occupations in the community.

While the summary data just presented offer important indications of the long-range trends in gross mobility, they provide no insights into the relative amounts of upward and downward movement. The latter analysis is essential for a full understanding of the degree of opportunity available in the community. That is, a society could conceivably experience declining rates of gross mobility and simultaneously enjoy both rising rates of upward movement and falling rates of downward mobility and consequently greater opportunity. In addition, such an examination which also encompasses urban to rural and rural to urban movement will give further insights into how mobility is affected by urbanization and industrialization. Tables 14 and 15 present data showing rates for these various types of mobility; percentages in the former are based on mobility tables using the fifteen-point occupational scale while data in the latter are based on tables using collapsed categories.

Results from both examinations show in addition to the sharp decline in gross mobility that rates of upward occupational movement decreased even more acutely. When finer occupational distinctions are used, these rates decline from 43.0 and 54.7 per cent respectively for the two decades before 1870 to 27.1 and 15.7 per cent in the following two time periods. These decreases become even more dramatic when collapsed occupational categories are employed falling from 33.0 and 26.3 per cent for the 1850's and 1860's to 7.2 and 5.2 per cent for the next two time periods. Equally important, throughout this period upward occupational mobility rates using collapsed occupational categories fall at a much faster rate than when finer occupational distinctions are employed. This would suggest that opportunity for substantial upward mobility declined more rapidly than did the possibilities for less significant movement.

While upward rates of mobility dropped, downward rates of mobility increased with 1870 again appearing to be the major turning point. In the two decades before 1870, regardless of the type of occupational classification used, the proportion downwardly mobile never exceeds 4 per cent. By contrast in the two decades after 1870, downward rates of mobility in all cases exceed 4 per cent. Using the fifteen-point occupational scale, the rates of downward movement are 10.7 and 16.0 per cent for the time periods 1870–1880 and 1880–1894 respectively. As with measures of gross and upward mobility, collapsed occupational categories show lower rates of downward mobility. This type of classification reveals downward rates of mobility of 4.1 per cent for the decade of the 1870's and 6.9 per cent for the 1880–1894 time period.

In contrast to upward and downward movement, no clear pattern emerges regarding rural to urban or urban to rural occupational mobility. Only in the 1850's, moreover, did these processes involve a large proportion of the labor force

TABLE 14

Types of Occupational Mobility Occurring in the Holland Community Using Fifteen Occupational Groups, 1850–1894

	1850–60	1850–70	1850–80	1860–70	1860–80	1870–80	1870–94	1880–94
Percentage Mobile	75.4	85.3	91.6	70.0	79.6	47.7	48.4	39.5
Percentage Upwardly Mobile	43.0	50.5	54.0	54.7	63.8	27.1	24.6	15.7
Percentage Downwardly Mobile	2.3	2.1	1.5	3.2	2.6	10.7	15.6	16.0
Percentage Urban to Rural	28.5	28.4	31.2	4.3	4.0	5.6	2.5	1.0
Percentage Rural to Urban	1.5	4.2	5.0	7.9	9.1	4.2	5.7	6.5

TABLE 15

Types of Occupational Mobility Occurring in the Holland Community Using Collapsed Occupational Groups, 1850–1894

	1850–60	1850–70	1850–80	1860–70	1860–80	1870–80	1870–94	1880–94
Percentage Mobile	64.4	76.5	80.7	39.6	47.9	21.2	23.8	19.6
Percentage Upwardly Mobile	33.0	42.5	44.5	26.3	33.1	7.2	9.0	5.2
Percentage Downwardly Mobile	1.5	1.4	0.0	1.1	1.6	4.1	6.6	6.9
Percentage Urban to Rural	28.5	28.4	31.2	4.3	4.0	5.6	2.5	1.0
Percentage Rural to Urban	1.5	4.2	5.0	7.9	9.1	4.2	5.7	6.5

of the Holland community. In that decade, 30 per cent of those remaining in the settlement moved from a rural to an urban occupation or vice versa; furthermore, the bulk of the total group (28.5 per cent) left an urban classification for a rural one. This rather high proportion seems due more to errors in the manuscripts of the federal census of 1850 than to any peculiar migration pattern. As pointed out earlier, it appears that an overwhelming majority of those listed in the census of 1850 as laborers could have more appropriately been designated "farmers without farms" or farm laborers. After 1860 rural to urban and urban to rural occupational movement was much lower and combined never exceeded one-eighth of the labor force. Further, in the three time periods following 1860, the two streams of movement do not follow a consistent pattern relative to each other, contrary to what might be expected given the community's greater reliance on a non-agricultural economy.

The analysis, thus far, indicates that the social structure of the Holland community, as measured by rates of gross mobility, upward movement, and Cramér V, became increasingly rigid, particularly after 1870. Moreover, using collapsed occupational categories, which offer a better measure of significant mobility than finer ones, reveals greater decreases in gross and upward mobility and increasingly stronger relationships between beginning and ending occupation than does the use of finer categories. By contrast, rates of downward mobility increase after 1870 regardless of the type of classification employed. That such changes correspond directly to decreasing rates of change in the occupational structure indicates that the development and establishment of the community stimulated greater changes in the occupational structure than did the beginnings of industrialism and consequently offered a greater impetus to gross and upward occupational mobility than did urbanization and industrialization.

III.

Although both gross and upward rates of mobility declined over time, opportunity for movement increased with the length of one's stay in the settlement. Using collapsed occupational categories reveals that of those who remained in the community between 1850 and 1860, slightly more than

60 per cent were mobile (see table 13). By contrast over 80 per cent of those within this group who stayed until 1880 experienced occupational movement. Likewise, the rate of movement for those listed in both the censuses of 1860 and 1880 surpassed the rate for those in the 1860–1870 group while a comparison of the data for the 1870–1880 and 1870–1894 samples yields comparable results. Moreover, the fifteen-point scale reveals a similar relationship between total mobility and length of stay in the community (see table 12). Thus, regardless of the type of occupational classification employed, the percentage rates of mobility support the contention that the opportunity for occupational mobility increased with one's lengthening duration in the community.

Similar to the pattern for gross mobility, one's chances for upward occupational movement increased with the length of residency in the community (see tables 14 and 15). That is, the portion of the group listed in the census of 1850 that remained in the community through 1870 and 1880 had a much higher percentage of upwardly mobile persons than did the entire group appearing in both the censuses of 1850 and 1860. This pattern also persists for those appearing in the census of 1860; those who remained until 1880 had a far higher rate of upward mobility than did those in the 1860–1870 group.

The exception to this pattern comes with the 1870 groups. Using the finer occupational grouping of fifteen, the data show a lower rate of upward mobility for the 1870–1894 than for the 1870–1880 group with the latter having an upward mobility rate of 2.5 per cent higher than the former. However, collapsed occupational categories indicate just the reversal of this process with the 1870–1894 group having a rate 1.8 per cent higher than the 1870–1880 one. It would seem then that in general the longer a person remained in a community the greater would be his chances not only for occupational mobility but also for upward movement. Such findings also offer further support for the contention in Chapter III that persistence rather than migration offered the more viable avenue for occupational mobility.

IV.

Comparing the rates of various occupational groups over time offers additional insights into the sources of decline of mobility in the Holland community and indicates the greatest source of decrease in gross mobility for any given decade accrued to either the blue-collar or rural-workers group (see table 16). Between the 1850's and the 1860's the proportion of blue-collar workers mobile fell 31 per cent; farm operators with a decline of slightly more than 20 per cent were the only other group suffering a decrease. Differentials in the rates of movement of various occupational groups between the decades of the 1860's and the 1870's show that only the rural workers group, with a decline of over 30 per cent, experienced a decrease in mobility. Because of the nature of the occupational data for 1894, it is only feasible to compare the mobility rates of those holding non-agricultural occupations in the 1880's with those in the 1870's. Such an analysis reveals that both blue-collar and white-collar workers suffered a decline in occupational movement. However, blue-collar rates, decreasing over 25 per cent, fell far faster than those of white-collar workers whose rates slipped less than 5 per cent. This examination suggests that as mobility declined as a result of the decrease in structural change those groups at the bottom of the occupational ladder saw their rates of mobility fall disproportionately faster than those at the top.

While the preceding analysis offers a general overview of gross mobility, the following examination will clarify both the specific rates of upward, downward, rural to urban and urban to rural movement of the various occupational categories and how these rates contribute to overall mobility pat-

TABLE 16

CHANGING RATES OF GROSS MOBILITY FOR OCCUPATIONAL GROUPS, 1850–1894

	1850–1860	1860–1870	1870–1880	1880–1894
White-collar	0.0	14.3	26.7	22.2
Blue-collar	69.0	38.0	38.2	10.4
Farm Operators	29.0	8.4	8.8	64.5*
Rural Workers	72.8	82.9	50.0	
Total Gross Rate of Mobility	64.4	39.6	21.2	19.6

* In this column, all agricultural workers are lumped together in one category because of the nature of the data.

terns. In addition, the relationship of vertical mobility to movement between the urban and rural sectors will be investigated. Furthermore, because the use of the fifteen occupational schema would greatly reduce the size of the samples, only the four major occupational groups will be included in this examination. Even using the broad groups, the small size of the samples in some cases necessitates caution regarding conclusions drawn from them.

Although displaying the lesser movement of the two urban groups, the proportion of white-collar workers mobile increased in the three decades following 1850 before declining slightly in the 1880–1894 time period (see table 17). That this pattern of increasing mobility runs counter to that found for the entire labor force does not mean that white-collar rates deviated significantly from the trends discerned for the entire community. Quite to the contrary, data on downward mobility into blue-collar positions clearly indicate that the growing inability of white-collar workers to retain their posi-

TABLE 17

MOBILITY RATES AND PATTERNS FOR URBAN WHITE-COLLAR WORKERS, 1850–1894

	Percentage Mobile	Downward to Blue-collar Workers	To Farm Operators	To Rural Workers
1850–60	0.0	0.0	0.0	0.0
	(0)[1]	(0)	(0)	(0)
1850–70	0.0	0.0	0.0	0.0
	(0)	(0)	(0)	(0)
1850–80	0.0	0.0	0.0	0.0
	(0)	(0)	(0)	(0)
1860–70	14.3	7.1	4.8	2.4
	(6)	(3)	(2)	(1)
1860–80	13.3	6.7	6.7	0.0
	(4)	(2)	(2)	(0)
1870–80	26.7	18.8	7.9	0.0
	(27)	(19)	(8)	(0)
1870–94	19.0	19.0	0.0	. .[2]
	(8)	(8)	(0)	. .
1880–94	22.2	21.2	1.0	. .
	(22)	(21)	(1)	. .

[1] Figures in parentheses indicate the absolute number involved.

[2] Data for 1894 employ only one agricultural category because of the nature of the 1894 census which makes it impossible to distinguish between farm operators and rural workers.

tions provided the major source of the increase in the community's downward mobility rate. These rates which are only
0.0 and 7.1 per cent for non-manual workers in the two decades prior to the 1870's jump dramatically to 18.8 and 21.2
per cent in the two periods following 1870. Such a pattern,
particularly the steep rises after 1870, corresponds directly
to that found for the entire labor force and indicates the
close association between the mobility patterns of white-collar workers and the mounting downward mobility found in
the community after the first two decades of settlement. In
addition to entering blue-collar occupations, a small proportion of white-collar workers entered the agricultural labor
force. As might be expected, the vast majority of these urban
to rural migrants became farm operators; only one of the
ten who made this move in the 1860's or 1870's became a
rural worker. Thus, entering agriculture for white-collar
workers merely entailed exchanging a position at or near
the top of the urban occupational hierarchy for one at or
near the top of the rural structure. Lastly, no significant differences in mobility patterns exist between those white-collar
workers listed in two successive censuses and those also enumerated in subsequent censuses.

To an even greater extent than their urban counterparts,
farm operators experienced low rates of occupational mobility. With the exception of the 1850's, their rates of movement
(8.4 and 8.8 per cent for the 1860's and 1870's respectively)
were one-fourth those of white collar workers (see table 18).[9]
That their mobility rates fell dramatically between the 1850's
and 1860's and then remained constant, however, differs
from the case of urban non-manual workers. Similarly, downward movement into the rural-workers category which drops
from over 16 per cent in the 1850's to 1.6 and 3.2 per cent
in the following two decades runs contrary to the pattern
exhibited by white-collar workers and further indicates that
the sharp increase in downward mobility after 1870 can be
directly attributed to urban non-manual workers. Although
the proportion of farm operators entering the urban labor
market follows no consistent pattern over time, farmers

---

[9] Because of the nature of the 1894 data, it is impossible to examine intra-generational mobility of both farm operators and rural workers beyond 1880.

TABLE 18

MOBILITY RATES AND PATTERNS FOR FARM OPERATORS, 1850–1894

	Percentage Mobile	To White-collar Worker	To Blue-collar Worker	Downward to Rural Workers
1850–60	29.0	0.0	12.9	16.1
	(9)[1]	(0)	(4)	(5)
1850–70	36.0	8.0	12.0	16.0
	(9)	(2)	(3)	(4)
1850–80	15.4	7.7	7.7	0.0
	(2)	(1)	(1)	(0)
1860–70	8.4	4.8	2.0	1.6
	(21)	(12)	(5)	(4)
1860–80	12.0	5.2	3.6	3.1
	(23)	(10)	(7)	(6)
1870–80	8.8	1.6	4.1	3.2
	(39)	(7)	(18)	(14)
1870–94	50.0	25.0	25.0	. .[2]
	(4)	(2)	(2)	. .
1880–94	62.5	25.0	37.5	. .
	(10)	(4)	(6)	. .

[1] Figures in parentheses indicate the absolute number involved.

[2] Data for 1894 employ only one agricultural category because of the nature of the 1894 census which makes it impossible to distinguish between farm operators and rural workers.

tended disproportionately to enter blue-collar positions in contrast to white-collar workers who almost always became farm operators when moving in the opposite direction. Excluding only the 1860's, the majority of farm operators entering the non-agricultural labor force became manual rather than non-manual workers. Lastly, no major differences appear in overall mobility patterns between farm operators enumerated in two successive censuses and those listed in one more than ten years later except for those mobility matrices based in part on 1894 census data which by their nature inflate rates of movement for all members of the agricultural labor force.

Rates of mobility for blue-collar workers exceed those of both white-collar workers and farm operators in every time period except for 1880–1894. More specifically, rates for blue-collar workers decrease more than 30 per cent (owing partly to the misclassification of laborers in the 1850 census) between the 1850's and 1860's, level off at about 38 per

cent in the following two decades, and then fall precipitously
to almost 10 per cent for the 1880–1894 period (see table
19). This suggests that the steep decline in gross mobility
for the entire labor force in the 1870's cannot be directly
attributed to changing rates of movement for blue-collar
workers. However, the dramatic reduction in their rate after
1880 helped to sustain the overall decline begun in the
1870's.

Except for changes between the 1850's and 1860's, rates
of upward mobility into the white-collar category follow a
pattern identical to that for gross mobility. After more than
doubling between the 1850's and 1860's, rates of upward
movement plateau at about 20 per cent before declining by
more than half in the 1880–1894 time period. Similar to
the trend for gross mobility, upward rates for blue-collar
workers indicate that the steep decline in upward movement
beginning in the 1870's is not directly traceable to mobility
from this category. However, decreases in upward movement

TABLE 19

MOBILITY RATES AND PATTERNS FOR URBAN BLUE-COLLAR WORKERS, 1850–1894

	Percentage Mobile	Upward into White-collar	To Farm Operators	To Rural Workers
1850–60	69.0	8.2	38.6	22.2
	(109)[1]	(13)	(61)	(35)
1850–70	72.7	16.1	53.1	3.5
	(104)	(23)	(76)	(5)
1850–80	79.0	16.0	58.0	5.0
	(79)	(16)	(58)	(5)
1860–70	38.0	19.4	14.7	3.9
	(49)	(25)	(19)	(5)
1860–80	48.9	29.3	16.3	3.3
	(45)	(27)	(15)	(3)
1870–80	38.2	20.1	14.7	3.4
	(78)	(41)	(30)	(7)
1870–94	20.6	16.2	4.4	. .[2]
	(14)	(11)	(3)	. .
1880–94	10.2	9.1	1.1	. .
	(18)	(16)	(2)	. .

[1] Figures in parentheses indicate the absolute number involved.

[2] Data for 1894 employ only one agricultural category because of the nature of
the 1894 census which makes it impossible to distinguish between farm operators
and rural workers.

after 1880, as with gross mobility, helped to sustain the overall pattern emerging in the previous decade.

Similar to white-collar workers, the vast majority of blue-
collar workers entering the agricultural labor force assumed
positions as farm operators rather than as rural workers. In
every decade between 1850 and 1880, at least 60 per cent
of blue-collar workers entering agriculture became farm operators. This suggests that, for a large number of manual
workers in the Holland community, entering agriculture
served as a viable avenue for upward mobility. Moreover,
if the proportion of blue-collar workers entering white-collar
positions is added to those becoming farm operators, the
percentage significantly improving their occupational status
was more than a third in every decade between 1850 and
1880.

Lastly, in contrast to both farm operators and white-collar
workers, mobility was greater for those blue-collar workers
appearing in a census more than ten years after their original
entry than for those enumerated in two successive decades.
The differential for those appearing in both the 1850 and
1860 census and for those enumerated in both 1850 and
1880 is 10 per cent; for those upwardly mobile into either
the white-collar group and/or the farm operators category,
the respective differentials are almost 8 and 20 per cent.
Similar patterns exist for those in both 1860 and 1870 and
1860 and 1880. Only for those listed in both the 1870 and
1880 and 1870 and 1894 censuses does this pattern break
down. Part of the reason for this may be that the 1894 census,
including only those living in the city of Holland, excludes
many blue-collar workers who may have entered the agricultural labor force. This, however, cannot account for the drop
in the proportion entering white-collar positions. Such findings suggest that a concomitant development to the decrease
in upward mobility for blue-collar workers was a decrease
in the chances for upward mobility with the length of one's
stay in the community.

Rural workers, in sharp contrast to farm operators who
were the least mobile group, displayed the greatest amount
of occupational movement in every decade from 1850 to
1880 (see table 20). Although the most mobile group, rural
workers' occupational movement declined precipitously after

TABLE 20

MOBILITY RATES AND PATTERNS FOR RURAL WORKERS, 1850–1894

	Proportion Mobile	Into White-collar	Into Blue-collar	Upward into Farm Operators
1850–60	72.8	0.0	0.7	72.1
	(99)[1]	(0)	(1)	(98)
1850–70	94.6	3.6	2.7	88.3
	(105)	(4)	(3)	(98)
1850–80	95.3	5.8	3.5	86.0
	(82)	(5)	(3)	(74)
1860–70	82.9	4.3	11.4	67.1
	(174)	(9)	(24)	(141)
1860–80	91.2	6.1	9.4	75.7
	(165)	(11)	(17)	(137)
1870–80	50.0	7.7	9.6	32.7
	(26)	(4)	(5)	(17)
1870–94	75.0	25.0	50.0	. .[2]
	(3)	(1)	(2)	. .
1880–94	66.7	13.3	53.3	. .
	(10)	(2)	(8)	. .

[1] Figures in parentheses indicate the absolute number involved.

[2] Data for 1894 employ only one agricultural category because of the nature of the 1894 census which makes it impossible to distinguish between farm operators and rural workers.

1870; in the two decades prior to that date, over 70 per cent were mobile compared with only 50 per cent during the 1870's. To a great extent this drop helps to explain the sharp decline denoted in overall mobility rates for the entire labor force. Rural workers also recorded the highest rates of upward mobility. Movement into the farm operator's category, moreover, steadily decreased with the 1870's recording the sharpest decline; in the 1850's and 1860's rates are 72.1 and 67.1 per cent respectively and only 32.7 per cent during the 1870's. Thus, this decrease in large part accounts for the sharp decline in upward movement for the entire labor force after 1870.

Similar to farm operators, rural workers entering the non-agricultural labor market usually secured manual rather than non-manual positions. In every time period the majority became blue-collar workers and except for the decade of the 1870's twice as many entered manual rather than non-manual pursuits. Thus, regardless of the specific occupation, members of the agricultural labor force who secured urban occu-

pations were most likely to assume positions in the lower
part of that occupational structure in contrast to urban workers who were far more likely to enter the agricutural labor
force as farm operators than as rural workers.

On the other hand, like blue-collar workers, rural workers
remaining in the community for more than one decade were
far more likely to experience both greater gross and upward
mobility than those listed in two successive censuses. Comparing those enumerated in both 1850 and 1860 with those
listed in 1850 and 1880, the differential in gross mobility
surpasses 20 per cent, and the difference in upward movement equals almost 14 per cent. Differentials in gross and
upward mobility for those listed in both 1860 and 1870 and
1860 and 1880 almost equals 10 per cent. Unfortunately,
the nature of the 1894 data prohibits a comparable analysis
for those enumerated in 1870.

The preceding analysis of mobility by occupational group
indicates that the steep decline in both rates of gross and
upward movement after 1870 for the entire labor force can
be attributed to the declining opportunity of rural workers.
This suggests the structural changes that accompanied high
rates of movement in the early years of settlement revolved
around the easy access to farm ownership. However, the
growing population of the community and the concomitant
declining land-man ratio restricted opportunity in agriculture. That urban blue-collar rates of upward and gross mobility decline sharply after 1880 further indicates that urbanization and industrialization offered no substantial alternative
avenue for increased movement. By contrast, the increase
in the downward mobility rate after 1870, which was most
clearly reflected in the behavior of white-collar workers, suggests the economic changes in the community after 1870
increased the likelihood that white-collar workers would be
unable to maintain their economic positions.

In addition to the occupational components of overall patterns of mobility for the entire labor force, some additional
trends emerge. Although not true for white-collar workers
and farm operators, blue-collar and rural workers each experienced both greater gross and upward movement as the
length of residency in the community increased. Blue-collar
and rural workers also had higher rates of mobility than did

white-collar workers and farm operators in all time periods except for 1880–1894. Furthermore, both groups and especially rural workers showed substantial upward movement. In all but one decade (the 1870's), at least two-thirds of the rural workers remaining in the community became farm operators and with the exception of the 1880–1894 time period, at least one-third of the blue-collar workers became either white-collar workers or farm operators. The disproportionately high out-migration rates of these groups, however, may have skewed the sample toward the most successful and thus partially accounts for the high rates of upward movement. By contrast, farm operators and non-manual workers remained less mobile. In only the 1870's were more than a quarter of the white-collar workers mobile and only the 1850's saw the proportion of farm operators changing occupations rise above 10 per cent.

The relationship between movement from a rural to an urban occupation and vice versa reveals two different tendencies. In every time period where it is possible to identify farm operators, the vast majority of urban workers entering rural occupations became farm operators. Thus urban to rural movement served primarily as an avenue of upward mobility for blue-collar workers while representing what may be construed as parallel movement for white-collar workers. In contrast, both farm operators and rural workers who entered urban job categories tended to become blue- rather than white-collar workers. Similar to the explanation for higher rates of out-migration for rural workers, the reason for this difference may be that marginal farm operators and particularly rural workers were being forced out of agricultural positions because of the changing economy of the community and the relatively declining prosperity of agriculture whereas the urban workers, particularly blue-collar, who moved into rural occupations only did so after they had accumulated sufficient resources to purchase a prosperous farm. These patterns have additional implications for understanding the mobility process in the Holland community. If, as Eric Lampard suggests, urbanization on one level can be conceptualized as the movement from agricultural to non-agricultural occupations, then the process of urbanization did not serve directly to increase the opportunity for economic advance-

TABLE 21
INTRA-GROUP MOBILITY PATTERNS OF FARM OPERATORS, 1850–1880

	1850–60	1860–70	1870–80
% Mobile	81.8	62.4	32.8
% Upwardly Mobile	77.3	62.0	24.2
% Downwardly			
Mobile	4.5	0.4	8.6
Total	22	229	405

ment in the Holland community. On the other hand, it offers additional support for the contention that the settlement and early development of the community offered greater opportunity for mobility than did the beginnings of urbanization and industrialization.[10]

Turning to a brief perusal of patterns of mobility for those remaining within each of the broad occupational classifications indicates that farm operators experienced the greatest mobility of any group within their specific classification (see table 21). Only in the 1870's did more than half of those remaining in this category not experience movement; almost all of the mobility, moreover, was upward owing to the rising value of farms as a result of farmers bringing higher proportions of their acreage under cultivation. This plus the stagnation of the agricultural sector of the community's economy also accounts for the decrease in intra-group mobility during the decade of the 1870's since by then most of the land had already been improved. That the rates of both gross and upward movement fell sharply after 1870 helps further to explain the precipitous decline in mobility for the entire labor force using fifteen occupational categories. In addition, downward rates, after falling to less than 1 per cent between the 1850's and 1860's, increase sharply in the 1870's. This last development, likewise, parallels the pattern for the entire labor force.

In contrast to farm operators, rural workers demonstrated far less mobility within their group than between broad occupational categories. In only one of the decades under consid-

[10] Lampard, 1965: pp. 519–522.

TABLE 22
INTRA-GROUP MOBILITY PATTERNS OF RURAL WORKERS, 1850–1880

	1850–60	1860–70	1870–80
% Mobile	18.9	36.1	23.1
% Upwardly Mobile	5.4	30.6	11.5
% Downwardly Mobile	13.5	5.6	11.5
Total	37	36	26

eration, 1860–1870, were more than one-third of those who remained in the rural workers category mobile (see table 22). More specifically, both rates of gross and upward movement rise between the 1850's and 1860's before falling in the 1870's and downward rates follow a reverse pattern. Thus only changes between the latter two decades parallel those for the entire labor force using the fifteen-point occupational schema.

Within the urban white-collar classification, likewise, very little intra-group mobility occurred (see table 23). No more than 34 per cent were mobile within this broad classification in any of the time periods between 1850 and 1894. Moreover, rates of gross, upward, and downward movement within this category do not follow the same pattern as rates for the entire labor force. Gross mobility show a slight but steady rise to 1880 before declining compared with a continuous decrease beginning in 1850 for the total labor force. Upward movement alternates between falling and rising between 1850 and 1894 instead of steadily declining after 1870. That downward mobility within the group steadily declines after 1870 also runs counter to the general mobility patterns.

TABLE 23
INTRA-GROUP MOBILITY PATTERNS OF URBAN WHITE-COLLAR WORKERS, 1850–1894

	1850–60	1860–70	1870–80	1880–94
% Mobile	25.0	25.0	33.8	11.7
% Upwardly Mobile	12.5	11.1	23.0	6.5
% Downwardly Mobile	12.5	13.9	10.8	5.2
Total	12	36	74	77

TABLE 24

INTRA-GROUP MOBILITY PATTERNS OF URBAN BLUE-COLLAR WORKERS, 1850–1894

	1850–60	1860–70	1870–80	1880–94
% Mobile	18.4	21.3	30.1	29.7
% Upwardly Mobile	18.4	15.0	24.6	17.1
% Downwardly Mobile	0.0	6.3	5.6	12.7
Total	59	80	126	158

As with the urban white-collar and rural workers there was comparatively little mobility within the urban blue-collar category (see table 24). No more than one-third of those remaining within this group between 1850 and 1894 were occupationally mobile. In contrast to overall mobility trends using the fifteen-point classification gross mobility steadily climb to 1880 before slightly decreasing after that date. Furthermore, rates after 1870 exceed those prior to 1870 indicating that mobility within this category tended to increase as the movement of blue-collar workers into other occupational categories diminished. Primarily this change resulted in increased movement of both skilled and unskilled workers into the semiskilled group after 1870 and thus reflected the growing importance of the factory in the economic life of the community.[11] Lastly, rates of upward and downward mobility rise and fall in the opposite direction of each other in every time period and consequently do not parallel trends for the entire labor force.

Occupational movement within broad occupational categories mirrored two major social and economic trends in the Holland community. Similar to the decline of inter-occupational group mobility for rural workers, decreasing rates of upward movement within the farm operators category reflected the relative decline in uncleared agricultural land and the economic stagnation of agriculture in general. Likewise, one manifestation of the community's increasing reliance on light industry was increased movement within the blue-collar

---

[11] The proportion of skilled and unskilled workers remaining in the blue-collar category who became semiskilled workers never exceeded 12 per cent in the 1850's and 1860's while exceeding 20 per cent in the 1870's.

group, particularly into the semiskilled category. Thus, although mobility within broad occupational groups did not parallel overall patterns of mobility for the entire labor force, it does reveal two trends that reflect major structural changes taking place in the community.

V.

To understand further the mobility process in the Holland community, the impact of both ethnicity and age, two variables which frequently affect rates and patterns of occupational movement, will next be investigated. That the Dutch-born and their offspring comprised over 90 per cent of samples for any given time period, however, puts certain limitations on controlling for ethnicity and necessitates that the major comparison of mobility be made between the Dutch- and non-Dutch-born.

Controlling for ethnicity does not reveal substantially different patterns of occupational movement. With the exception of the first decade under consideration, gross rates of mobility for the Dutch-born and non-Dutch-born do not differ by more than 2 per cent (see table 25). It should be pointed out, however, that in the first decade only seven people in the labor force were not born in The Netherlands. In addition, no great differences exist in the rates of upward

TABLE 25

PATTERNS OF INTRA-GENERATIONAL OCCUPATIONAL MOBILITY OF DUTCH-BORN AND NON-DUTCH-BORN USING COLLAPSED OCCUPATIONAL CATEGORIES, 1850–1894

	1850–60		1860–70		1870–80		1880–94	
	Dutch	non-Dutch	Dutch	non-Dutch	Dutch	non-Dutch	Dutch	non-Dutch
% Mobile	64.8	42.9	39.6	40.0	21.2	21.7	19.0	20.5
% Upwardly Mobile	32.7	42.9	26.4	25.0	7.5	4.8	3.9	7.1
% Downwardly Mobile	1.5	0.0	1.0	2.5	4.3	2.4	7.8	5.5
% Urban to Rural	29.1	0.0	3.9	10.0	5.4	7.2	1.7	0.0
% Rural to Urban	1.5	0.0	8.3	2.5	3.9	7.2	5.6	7.9
Total	330	7	591	40	718	83	179	127

or downward mobility between the groups after 1860 with the differences never surpassing 4 per cent. Even though the differentials between the two groups are greater for urban to rural and rural to urban occupational movement than for other types of mobility, no consistent pattern emerges to suggest that one group differed substantially from another. Thus, it seems safe to conclude that little relationship existed between ethnicity and occupational mobility in the Holland community. Although such a relationship might be found to exist if the non-Dutch-born were broken down into specific ethnic groups, the small number in these sub-samples precludes such an examination.

In contrast to ethnicity, employing age cohorts yields substantially different patterns of mobility (see table 26). During the 1870's, the time period with the largest sample, an inverse relationship existed between age and mobility, gross rates of mobility steadily decrease as the age of the cohort increases. In this relationship, moreover, age thirty represents a breaking point with rates for those under thirty almost double those for every age group over thirty. Furthermore, with the exception of the youngest cohort which includes only nineteen individuals, both upward and downward mobility rates follow similar patterns. By contrast, no discernible trends appear for either urban to rural or rural to urban movement.

While this examination of intra-generational mobility has concentrated on occupational movement in one immigrant

TABLE 26

SUMMARY MOBILITY DATA BY AGE COHORTS FOR THE HOLLAND COMMUNITY USING COLLAPSED OCCUPATIONAL CATEGORIES, 1870–1880

	11–20	21–30	31–40	41–50	51–60	Data for Total Sample
Gross Mobility	42.1	36.0	19.9	16.1	14.7	21.2
Upward Mobility	0.0	16.5	9.7	5.0	1.3	7.2
Downward Mobility	5.3	6.5	3.5	3.2	3.3	4.1
Urban to Rural Mobility	26.3	8.6	4.0	5.0	3.3	5.6
Rural to Urban Mobility	10.5	4.3	2.7	2.8	6.7	4.2
Total	19	139	226	218	150	

community, it has so far overlooked the relationship between emigration from The Netherlands to America and occupational mobility. Such an analysis, however, is possible because between 1846 and 1877 the Dutch government collected data on occupation, religion, age, and marital and economic status for all those emigrating. This information makes it possible to trace the occupational careers of a number of the residents of the Holland community back to their native land and thus gain some insight to the relationship between occupational mobility and immigration.

For those whose occupational careers could be traced back to The Netherlands, substantial occupational mobility accompanied migration to America. Table 27 presents rates and patterns of mobility based on a comparison of the occupations in The Netherlands of immigrants, grouped according to the decade of their departure, and their occupations as enumerated in the various censuses of the Holland community. In only one case (those who left The Netherlands between 1850 and 1859 and were enumerated in the census of 1870), did fewer than half of any group of immigrants fall into the same broad occupational category to which they belonged in The Netherlands. On all other occasions, at least half and more commonly 60 per cent or more experienced occupational movement.

In almost every instance, movement from an urban to a rural occupation supplied the major source of mobility. This type of movement accounted for almost half of the entire mobility for all groups in every decade between 1850 and 1880. By contrast, the reverse process, that is, movement from rural to urban occupations represented a far smaller proportion of the total mobility; in only one case did more than 5 per cent of a group experience this type of movement.

A closer inspection of the movement from an urban occupation in The Netherlands to a rural one in Holland indicates that this was the major avenue of upward mobility. For every group of immigrants leaving The Netherlands between 1846 and 1869, a substantial portion left urban blue-collar positions in the old country to become farm operators in the New World. Although the 1850 census reveals that only 3.3 per cent became farm operators, the next three censuses record 27.4, 43.9, and 46.8 per cent respectively of the blue-

TABLE 27

SUMMARY OCCUPATIONAL MOBILITY DATA FOR THOSE LIVING IN THE HOLLAND COMMU-
NITY FOR WHOM OCCUPATIONAL DATA FROM THE NETHERLANDS WERE AVAILABLE
USING COLLAPSED OCCUPATIONAL CATEGORIES

	1850	1860	1870	1880
Those leaving The Netherlands before 1850				
Percentage Mobile	60.0	68.5	64.9	70.2
Percentage Upwardly Mobile	2.2	6.8	8.8	10.6
Percentage Downwardly Mobile	25.6	9.6	3.5	0.0
Percentage Urban to Rural	28.9 (3.3)*	49.3 (27.4)*	50.9 (43.9)*	55.3 (46.8)*
Percentage Rural to Urban	3.3	2.7	1.8	4.3
Sample	90	73	57	47
Those leaving between 1850 and 1859				
Percentage Mobile		55.0	36.4	64.3
Percentage Upwardly Mobile		0.0	4.5	35.7
Percentage Downwardly Mobile		10.0	0.0	0.0
Percentage Urban to Rural		45.0 (10.0)*	31.8 (27.3)*	28.6 (28.6)*
Percentage Rural to Urban		0.0	0.0	0.0
Sample		20	22	14
Those leaving between 1860 and 1869				
Percentage Mobile			56.7	53.8
Percentage Upwardly Mobile			10.0	3.8
Percentage Downwardly Mobile			6.7	7.7
Percentage Urban to Rural			23.3 (20.0)*	38.5 (38.5)*
Percentage Rural to Urban			16.7	3.8
Sample			30	26

* Figures in parentheses represent the proportion of immigrants who moved from an urban blue-collar position in The Netherlands to the farm operators category in the Holland Community.

collar workers who migrated before 1850 as farm owners. Likewise those emigrating during the 1850's and the 1860's reveal a similar pattern; the proportion of those in each group who were blue-collar workers in The Netherlands and farm operators in the Holland community surpassed 25 per cent in 1880. From this analysis it is evident that mobility from an urban occupation in The Netherlands to a rural one in the Holland community was a major avenue of upward mobility.

Although movement from urban to rural occupations comprised the bulk of the mobility for those whose occupations could be traced back to The Netherlands, significant amounts of upward and downward movement also occurred. These types of mobility followed comparable patterns for those emigrating in the 1840's and 1850's with upward movement increasing and downward movement decreasing with each successive decade. Those who emigrated during the 1860's followed the reverse pattern, however, with the number of upwardly mobile decreasing and the proportion downwardly mobile increasing slightly between 1870 and 1880. Furthermore, this trend of decreasing opportunity over time for those who emigrated during the 1860's mirrors general patterns of opportunity in the community after 1870. Yet in spite of these decreases in opportunity for later immigrants, rates of upward mobility and movement from the blue-collar category to the farm operators group, suggest that emigration to America resulted in substantial improvement in the economic position of a large number of Dutch immigrants although once again the limited sample size requires extreme caution regarding this conclusion.

VI.

This analysis of mobility has indicated several patterns of intra-generational movement in one nineteenth-century community. High rates of both gross and upward mobility, particularly for rural workers and blue-collar workers who remained, characterized this newly settled community. In addition, data on immigrants from The Netherlands further suggest that immigration to the Holland community offered substantial opportunities for occupational mobility.

Perhaps the most significant result of this examination is

that rates of mobility declined as the community urbanized and industrialized. It is particularly important in this regard that mobility between broad occupational categories fell even more rapidly than did the observed mobility using finer occupational distinctions. Likewise rates of upward movement decreased, particularly after 1870, and at higher rates than gross mobility with collapsed occupational categories providing the clearest illustration of this trend while downward mobility rose after 1870. Thus opportunity in the Holland community diminished as the twentieth century approached. That smaller changes in the community's occupational structure after 1870 than before offers the best explanation for the decline in both mobility and opportunity further suggests that the settlement and early development of the community, including the clearing of unoccupied land, provided a greater impetus for occupational mobility than did subsequent urbanization and industrialization.

A closer inspection of movement by occupational groups offers additional insights into the pattern of decreasing opportunity within the community. Declining mobility for rural workers directly accounted for the initial overall decreases in both gross and upward movement in the 1870's. Similarly, gross and upward mobility fell after 1870 for those remaining within the farm-operators category indicating that declining opportunity in the agricultural sector occurred concomitantly with urbanization and industrialization. That decreasing blue-collar rates sustained these trends of falling mobility after 1880 and that white-collar workers most fully accounted for increasing downward movement after 1870 further indicate that the community's movement away from a rural-based economy did not offer the same opportunities for advancement as did the settlement and early development of the community.

The examination of rural to urban and urban to rural occupational movement further suggests that the process of urbanization in the community did not directly lead to greater opportunity for upward occupational mobility. Of the blue-collar and white-collar workers entering agriculture, a large majority became farm operators. By contrast, more than half of both the farm operators and rural workers who entered the urban labor force became blue-collar workers. This latter trend, which represents one conception of urbanization, suggests that the process of urbanization did not directly increase economic opportunity.

Lastly, within the broad occupational categories far less mobility took place than between the broad occupational groups. This was true for both urban categories and rural workers while farm operators provided the only exception to the pattern. Moreover, ethnicity in this largely homogeneous community did not affect mobility. By contrast age significantly altered rates of movement as those in the younger age brackets experienced far greater mobility than those over thirty.

V. Patterns of Inter-generational Occupational Movement in the Holland Community

I.

WHILE intra-generational mobility provides one indicator of the openness of a society, it is not the only means by which the fluidity of a social structure can be measured. Inter-generational mobility provides a second and perhaps equally important yardstick for appraising both the amount of mobility and the opportunity extant in a social order. The importance of this second measurement can quickly be illustrated. One could easily conceive of a society in which a great deal of intra-generational mobility occurred but where the occupational career of the next generation was almost completely determined by fathers' occupations. Any evaluation of the openness of such a society that ignores the relationship between father's and son's occupation, therefore, would be misleading.

The fact that nineteenth-century success literature was not only optimistic about one's chances of improving his own economic position but also equally enthusiastic about the future of the next generation further underscores the need for an analysis of inter-generational mobility. Thus, for the man who had been unable to move up the occupational hierarchy, there was always the consolation that his son would be able to achieve economic goals unobtainable for himself. That such aspirations were not foreign to Americans is indicated by the number of admonishments appearing in the self-help literature to parents on how to prepare their children for a successful career.[1]

---

[1] For a discussion of the nineteenth-century success literature, see Cawelti, 1965: *passim;* and Wyllie, 1954: *passim.*

To what extent then were the sons of the residents of the Holland community tied to the occupations of their fathers? Moreover, did the relationship between father's and son's occupation grow stronger in the latter years of the nineteenth century as rates of intra-generational mobility declined? The answer to these and similar questions will provide clearer guidelines with which to evaluate the openness of the community's social structure, to examine the impact of urbanization and industrialization on the social structure of a recently established community, and to draw some conclusions about late nineteenth-century American society.

The measurement of inter-generational mobility poses far more complex methodological considerations than does the estimation of intra-generational movement. In the latter, a comparison of the individual's occupation at two different points in his career is sought while the former involves a comparison between father's and son's occupation. The problem then becomes, at what stage in the careers of the two individuals is this analysis most appropriate? This question is particularly acute with regard to the career of the son. A large portion of the sons in the Holland community entered the labor force in their teens or early twenties and it is reasonable to assume that they took positions in the occupational hierarchy both far lower and different than they would ultimately hold. The examination of intra-generational mobility which reveals that the highest rates of occupational mobility occurred among those under thirty years of age supports this assumption. Moreover, a study of occupational mobility in Oakland, California, showing that over one-half of the white-collar workers at one time held manual positions further underscores this point and emphasizes the need to compare the occupations of two individuals at similar stages in their careers.[2] A partial solution to this problem can be achieved by controlling for the age of sons and concentrating the examination of inter-generational mobility on sons over thirty years of age since it is reasonable to assume that by this age a higher level of occupational stability would have been achieved than for a younger group.

Summary mobility data for the Holland community further

---

[2] Lipset and Bendix, 1964: p. 168.

TABLE 28

SUMMARY RATES OF INTER-GENERATIONAL MOBILITY FOR FATHERS AND SONS
APPEARING IN THE SAME CENSUS CONTROLLING FOR AGE, 1850–1894

	Under 20 (15–24)*	21–30 (25–34)*	31–40 (35–44)*	41–50 (45–54)*	51–60 (55–64)*	Average (Gross Mobility Rates)	Sample Size
1850	23.1 (3)	52.4 (11)	57.1 (4)	. .	. .	43.9 (18)	41
1860	66.7 (34)	47.9 (23)	52.9 (9)	100.0 (2)	. .	58.0 (69)	119
1870	58.3 (7)	60.4 (29)	62.5 (20)	50.0 (4)	. .	61.2 (63)	103
1880	71.8 (84)	73.6 (134)	60.8 (31)	62.5 (10)	100.0 (3)	71.2 (264)	371
1894	19.8 (16)	23.5 (8)	33.3 (4)	. .	. .	21.1 (28)	133

* Ages in parentheses represent age cohorts for those sons listed in 1894. Numbers in parentheses denote actual number belonging to cells. In this and all subsequent tables in this chapter, mobility rates will be based on the four collapsed occupational categories employed in Chapter IV. Totals of rows may not add up because of a few individuals whose birth dates were illegible.

illustrate that controlling for the age of sons and focusing attention on those over thirty offer a more complete picture of inter-generational movement. This method of comparing the occupations of fathers and sons appearing in the same census with the sons classified according to age yields quite different patterns of mobility than when only overall mobility rates are employed (see table 28). During these years, average gross mobility steadily increased between 1850 and 1880 before falling precipitously in the last time period.[3] Although gross rates declined sharply for all age cohorts between 1880 and 1894, they varied by age group between 1850 and 1880. The proportion of sons under twenty mobile increased rapidly from 1850 to 1880 with only a slight decrease in 1870.

___

[3] Rates for the 1894 census were substantially lower in large part because these data include only employed males residing in the city of Holland and therefore omit the vast majority of those employed in agricultural occupations. Such omissions would subsequently reduce rural to urban and urban to rural occupational movement, thus having the effect of diminishing gross rates of mobility in general. However, even when this factor is taken into consideration, gross rates of mobility declined substantially after 1880. Eliminating rural to urban and urban to rural occupational mobility reveals that rates of mobility for the 1880 group was 50.1 per cent compared to 18.8 per cent for the 1894 sample.

Similarly, with the exception of 1860, rates of movement for sons in the twenty-one to thirty age group steadily rose in the same years. By contrast, sons in the thirty-one to forty group saw their rates of mobility fluctuate within 10 per cent of each other. Thus, the increments in the overall gross rate of inter-generational mobility to 1880 resulted primarily from the increases accruing to those in the under thirty age group. Moreover, for this age group, almost all of this movement consisted of either urban to rural, rural to urban, or downward occupational mobility. If anything, then, such findings would indicate that, although gross mobility increased, the opportunity for economic improvement gradually diminished after 1850. However, both the variation in these data by age group and what is known of the rates of intra-generational mobility of those under thirty imply both that such a conclusion may be erroneous and that the best means of examining inter-generational mobility would be to concentrate on sons over thirty years of age.

In addition to controlling for son's age, using father's occupation at a point somewhat earlier in time than the son increases the likelihood that father's and son's occupation will be compared at similar stages in their careers. Ideally, then, it would be best to compare father's occupation in 1850, for example, with the occupations of sons over thirty in 1870. Such an examination would increase the probability of comparing two individuals' occupations at reasonably similar points in their careers.

Although ideal, this type of analysis does have some serious limitations. One major defect is that it greatly reduces the size of the sample for examining inter-generational mobility. The acquisition of a more representative group, however, offsets this loss of a sizable segment of the sample. A second weakness of this method is that it limits the efficacy of the investigation for analyzing long-range trends in inter-generational mobility. If son's occupation is compared with that of his father's at a point twenty years earlier, then 1870 would be the earliest date that occupational data pertaining to the son could be used; thus, it would reduce the number of observations for gauging trends in inter-generational movement from five to three. Consequently, in order to avoid some of these shortcomings, the occupations of sons over thirty will be compared to those of their fathers appearing in the same census and in the preceding census as well as in the one twenty years earlier. Thus with these three sub-samples, it will be possible to make some estimates of the changing rates of inter-generational mobility over longer periods of time while keeping in mind that at times father's and son's occupations will not be compared at similar stages in their careers.

II.

Centering the examination of inter-generational occupational mobility on those sons in the thirty-one to forty age group indicates that both mobility and opportunity diminished with the approach of the twentieth century. Both gross mobility and upward movement tend to decline while downward mobility tends to increase over time and in most cases the decade of the 1870's marked the most significant turning point. In addition, movement from an urban to a rural occupation became far less common and the reverse process became more widespread. Such patterns persisted regardless of whether the son's occupation is compared with that of his father in the same census, one ten years earlier, or one twenty years earlier (see tables 29–31).

Rates of gross mobility reveal a general decline which is especially pronounced for those sons whose occupations are compared with those of their fathers at an earlier date. For sons appearing in the same census as their fathers, gross rates fluctuate within 10 per cent of each other between 1850 and 1880 before declining drastically after 1880.[4] On the other hand, rates of inter-generational mobility for those sons appearing in a census later than their fathers clearly indicate steadily decreasing rates of occupational movement with the 1870's marking the major turning point. For those sons listed in a census ten years later than their fathers, rates of mobility fall only slightly between 1860 and 1870, drop 10 per cent in the next decade and then level off at about 50 per cent. A similar pattern existed for those enumerated twenty years after their fathers—a drop of slightly more than 10 per cent

---

[4] As noted above, part of this drop can be explained by the nature of the data for 1894. However, eliminating urban to rural and rural to urban mobility does not eliminate the difference in rates of mobility.

TABLE 29

PATTERNS OF INTER-GENERATIONAL MOBILITY FOR SONS AGES 31–40 APPEARING IN
THE SAME CENSUS AS THEIR FATHERS, 1850–1894

	1850	1860	1870	1880	1894[1]		Average[2] 1894
Percentage Mobile	57.1	52.9	62.5	60.8	23.5	33.3	28.4
Percentage Upwardly Mobile	0.0	35.3	28.1	9.8	2.9	8.3	5.6
Percentage Downwardly Mobile	42.9	5.9	15.6	27.5	17.6	16.7	17.2
Percentage Urban to Rural	14.3	11.8	6.3	9.8	0.0	0.0	0.0
Percentage Rural to Urban	0.0	0.0	12.5	13.7	2.9	8.3	5.6
Sample	7	17	32	51	34	12	

[1] Figures on the left-hand side of this column in this and subsequent tables denote sons in the 25–34 age bracket while those on the right-hand side are for sons in the 35–44 age group.

[2] The percentages for the two groups in this and subsequent tables were weighted equally even though the number of sons in the 25–34 age bracket was usually larger than the number in the 35–44 group. The reason for this procedure is that it would give a better indication of the rates of mobility for the 31–40 age group in 1894. If the size of the sample had been taken into consideration, then, the 25–34 group's average would have carried more weight and people under the age of 30 within the group who were over-represented would have skewed the average.

between 1870 and 1880 followed by a plateauing at about 55 per cent.

Perhaps even more importantly, rates of upward mobility fall precipitously after 1870. For sons and fathers in the same census, rates rise sharply in the 1850's and then continually decline with the 1870's recording the largest decrease (almost 20 per cent). A similar pattern characterized the movement of sons listed ten years later—a slight increase in the 1860's followed by a sharp drop (over 25 per cent) in the ensuing decade and then a leveling off between 1880 and 1894. Similarly, upward rates of movement fall almost 20 per cent between 1870 and 1880 for those sons enumerated twenty years later than their fathers and then decline only slightly after 1880.

TABLE 30

PATTERNS OF INTER-GENERATIONAL MOBILITY FOR SONS AGES 31–40 APPEARING IN
A CENSUS TEN YEARS LATER THAN THEIR FATHERS, 1850–1894

	Fathers 1850 Sons 1860	Fathers 1860 Sons 1870	Fathers 1870 Sons 1880	Fathers 1880 Sons 1894*		Average Fathers 1880 Sons 1894
Percentage Mobile	65.0	63.4	50.8	46.3	51.4	48.9
Percentage Upwardly Mobile	25.0	31.7	4.8	6.0	5.7	5.9
Percentage Downwardly Mobile	10.0	9.8	20.6	19.4	14.3	16.9
Percentage Urban to Rural	30.0	7.3	6.3	0.0	2.9	1.5
Percentage Rural to Urban	0.0	14.6	19.0	20.9	28.6	24.8
Sample	20	41	63	67	35	

* Figures on the left-hand side of this column denote sons in the 25–34 age bracket while those on the right-hand side are for sons in the 35–44 age group.

TABLE 31

PATTERNS OF INTER-GENERATIONAL MOBILITY FOR SONS AGES 31–40 APPEARING IN
A CENSUS TWENTY YEARS LATER THAN THEIR FATHERS, 1850–1894

	Fathers 1850 Sons 1870	Fathers 1860 Sons 1880	Fathers 1870 Sons 1894*		Average Fathers 1870 Sons 1894
Percentage Mobile	66.7	55.4	47.4	68.4	57.9
Percentage Upwardly Mobile	36.1	17.9	7.0	18.4	12.7
Percentage Downwardly Mobile	2.8	14.2	19.3	18.4	18.9
Percentage Urban to Rural	22.2	1.8	0.0	0.0	0.0
Percentage Rural to Urban	5.6	21.4	21.1	31.6	26.8
Sample	36	56	57	38	

* Figures on the left-hand side of this column denote sons in the 25–34 age bracket while those on the right-hand side are for sons in the 35–44 age group.

On the other hand, the proportion of downwardly mobile tended to increase with the 1870's recording the greatest change. As with rates of gross mobility, this pattern is the least pronounced for fathers and sons appearing in the same census. Downward movement falls dramatically during the 1850's, rises by about 10 per cent in each of the two following decades, and then between 1880 and 1894 declines to almost the same level that existed in 1870. By contrast, rates for sons appearing in a census later than their fathers reveal much clearer patterns of increased downward movement. Sons enumerated ten years later than their fathers experienced almost identical rates in the 1850's and 1860's followed by a sharp increase (10 per cent) the following decade and only a slight decline after 1880. Likewise, where father's and sons's occupations are compared twenty years apart, rates steadily increase with the 1870's recording the largest gain.

Urban to rural and rural to urban inter-generational movement display contrary tendencies. Regardless of the type of father-son comparison made, mobility from an urban to a rural occupation steadily decreased with the exception of fathers and sons appearing in the same census between 1870 and 1880. Just the reverse characterizes movement from a rural to an urban occupation; only fathers and sons enumerated in the same census between 1880 and 1894 offer an exception to this pattern. This deviation, however, can be attributed to the 1894 data including only the city of Holland which by its nature underestimates both rural to urban and urban to rural movement. Thus, to an even greater extent than patterns of intra-generational mobility, inter-generational trends of rural to urban and urban to rural mirrored the changing orientation of the community's economy away from agriculture.

The above examination of inter-generational mobility indicates that the social structure of the Holland community became increasingly rigid in the latter decades of the nineteenth century. Sons generally experienced less gross and upward movement after 1870 than before regardless of whether son's occupation is compared with his father's in the same year or over longer periods of time. This also shows that not only did mobility diminish but also the opportunity for economic advancement became less certain. In contrast to the

decline in upward movement, the probability that a son would
hold an occupational position lower than his father steadily
increased particularly after 1870. Lastly, increasing rural to
urban and decreasing urban to rural movement over time
reflected the increasing importance of an urban economy
to the Holland community.

III.

Similar to part of the examination of intra-generational
mobility investigating the mobility patterns of various occupational groups, controlling for the occupation of the father
is helpful in both understanding the mobility process and
determining the openness of a social structure. Controlling
for father's occupation, although revealing variations in the
patterns of movement of sons originating from different economic groups, yields somewhat small samples and consequently necessitates caution regarding conclusions drawn
from them. Yet, even with small samples, some general estimates of the trends and patterns of occupational mobility
of the offspring of fathers holding different occupations can
be made.

A large proportion of white-collar workers' sons occupied
positions different from those of their fathers; fewer than
half the total number in any of the sub-samples became white-
collar workers (see tables 32–34). On the other hand, al-

TABLE 32

INTER-GENERATIONAL PATTERNS OF MOBILITY FOR SONS (AGES 31–40) OF URBAN
WHITE-COLLAR WORKERS APPEARING IN THE SAME CENSUS AS THEIR FATHERS,
1850–1894

	1850	1860	1870	1880	1894*		Average 1894	Total
White-collar	0.0	0.0	0.0	50.0	57.1	60.0	58.6	48.4
Blue-collar	100.0	0.0	100.0	25.0	42.9	40.0	41.5	45.2
Farm Operators	0.0	0.0	0.0	12.5	0.0	0.0	0.0	3.2
Rural Workers	0.0	0.0	0.0	12.5	. .	. .	. .	3.2
Sample	1	0	3	8	14	5	19	31

* Left-hand column denotes those in the 25–34 age group and the right-hand
column those in the 35–44 age bracket. Agriculture data in this and subsequent
tables of this nature for 1894 lump all those employed in agriculture into one
category because no census of agriculture exists in order to differentiate farm operators from rural workers.

TABLE 33

INTER-GENERATIONAL MOBILITY PATTERNS FOR SONS (AGES 31–40) OF URBAN WHITE-
COLLAR WORKERS APPEARING IN A CENSUS TEN YEARS LATER THAN THEIR FATHERS,
1850–1894

	Fathers 1850 Sons 1860	Fathers 1860 Sons 1870	Fathers 1870 Sons 1880	Fathers 1880 Sons 1894*		Average Fathers 1880 Sons 1894	Total
White-collar	0.0	33.3	50.0	31.6	50.0	40.8	40.0
Blue-collar	0.0	66.7	25.0	68.4	50.0	59.2	55.0
Farm Operators	0.0	0.0	25.0	0.0	0.0	0.0	5.0
Rural Workers	0.0	0.0	0.0	. .	. .	. .	0.0
Sample	0	3	8	19	10	29	40

* Left-hand side of the column denotes those in the 25–34 age group and the
right-hand side those in the 35–44 age bracket.

though the small decadal samples make it difficult to detect
any firm trends, a slight tendency existed for these sons,
particularly when their occupations are compared with those
of their fathers in the same census, increasingly to occupy
white-collar positions with the passage of time. Thus, white-
collar sons' rates of movement tend to mirror the overall
decreasing rates of gross inter-generational mobility.

As these low rates of occupational inheritance might suggest, a substantial proportion of white-collar sons (ranging
from 45 to over 60 per cent) experienced downward mobility

TABLE 34

INTER-GENERATIONAL MOBILITY PATTERNS FOR SONS (AGES 31–40) OF URBAN WHITE-
COLLAR WORKERS APPEARING IN A CENSUS TWENTY YEARS LATER THAN THEIR
FATHERS, 1850–1894

	Fathers 1850 Sons 1870	Fathers 1860 Sons 1880	Fathers 1870 Sons 1894*		Average Fathers 1870 Sons 1894	Total
White-collar	33.3	0.0	38.9	22.2	30.6	31.3
Blue-collar	33.3	50.0	61.1	77.8	69.5	62.5
Farm Operators	33.3	50.0	0.0	0.0	0.0	6.3
Rural Workers	0.0	0.0	. .	. .	. .	0.0
Sample	3	2	18	9	27	32

* Left-hand column denotes those in the 25–34 age group and the right-hand
column those in the 35–44 age bracket.

into blue-collar positions. In addition, the percentage downwardly mobile varied directly with the time differential employed in comparing fathers' and sons' occupations; the total
proportion following this path increased with the length of
time elapsing between the father-son comparison. Thus,
when comparisons are made at more comparable points in
their careers, the son's high rate of downward movement
was even greater. Furthermore, these rates tend to increase
over time and especially for sons enumerated twenty years
later. The small samples again, however, require caution regarding these last two observations. In addition, a small number (6) entered the agricultural labor force and all but one
of these became farm operators. This is comparable to the
pattern of intra-generational mobility for white-collar workers who entered agriculture. Aside from this similarity, comparing these results with patterns of intra-generational movement indicates that white-collar workers experienced far less
downward movement than did their sons.

In contrast to the sons of non-manual workers, blue-collar
workers' sons had the highest rate of occupational inheritance
of any group (see tables 35–37). Seventy per cent of those
enumerated in the same census or one ten years later remained immobile while more than 60 per cent of those listed
twenty years later followed the same course. Furthermore,
with one exception (fathers and sons listed in the same census
between 1850 and 1860 and including only six people) the
proportion remaining blue-collar workers steadily rose regardless of the type of comparison made. The behavior of

TABLE 35

INTER-GENERATIONAL PATTERNS OF MOBILITY FOR SONS (AGES 31–40) OF URBAN BLUE-
COLLAR WORKERS APPEARING IN THE SAME CENSUS AS THEIR FATHERS, 1850–1894

	1850	1860	1870	1880	1894*		Average 1894	Total
White-collar	0.0	33.3	50.0	7.7	5.2	16.7	10.5	14.0
Blue-collar	66.7	0.0	16.7	69.2	94.7	83.3	89.0	70.0
Farm Operators	0.0	0.0	33.3	23.1	0.0	0.0	0.0	10.0
Rural Workers	33.3	66.7	0.0	0.0	. .	. .	. .	6.0
Sample	3	3	6	13	19	6	25	50

* Left-hand column denotes those in the 25–34 age group and the right-hand
column those in the 35–44 age bracket.

TABLE 36

INTER-GENERATIONAL MOBILITY PATTERNS FOR SONS (AGES 31–40) OF URBAN BLUE-
COLLAR WORKERS APPEARING IN A CENSUS TEN YEARS LATER THAN THEIR FATHERS,
1850–1894

	Fathers 1850 Sons 1860	Fathers 1860 Sons 1870	Fathers 1870 Sons 1880	Fathers 1880 Sons 1894[1]		Average Fathers 1880 Sons 1894	Total[2]
White-collar	0.0	14.3	11.1	12.1	15.4	13.7	11.8
Blue-collar	0.0	42.9	66.7	87.9	76.9	82.4	70.6
Farm Operators	50.0	42.9	22.2	0.0	7.7	3.9	11.8
Rural Workers	50.0	0.0	0.0	. .	. .	. .	4.4
Sample	6	7	9	33	13	46	68

[1] Left-hand side of the column denotes those in the 25–34 age group and the right-hand side those in the 35–44 age bracket.
[2] Other agricultural occupations equal 1.5 per cent.

blue-collar workers' sons, then, helps to account for the decline in inter-generational mobility after 1870 in the community.

For those sons leaving the blue-collar category, the most frequent type of movement was upward into a white-collar position. Those enumerated twenty years later than their fathers, moreover, had by far the largest total proportion (over 25 per cent) moving in this direction while no more than 14 per cent of the total in either of the other two groups

TABLE 37

INTER-GENERATIONAL MOBILITY PATTERNS FOR SONS (AGES 31–40) OF URBAN BLUE-
COLLAR WORKERS APPEARING IN A CENSUS TWENTY YEARS LATER THAN THEIR
FATHERS, 1850–1894

	Fathers 1850 Sons 1870	Fathers 1860 Sons 1880	Fathers 1870 Sons 1894*		Average Fathers 1870 Sons 1894	Total
White-collar	21.4	33.3	16.0	46.7	31.4	26.7
Blue-collar	28.6	66.7	84.0	53.3	68.7	61.7
Farm Operators	42.9	0.0	0.0	0.0	0.0	10.0
Rural Workers	7.1	0.0	. .	. .	. .	1.7
Sample	14	6	25	15	40	60

* Left-hand column denotes those in the 25–34 age group and the right-hand column those in the 35–44 age bracket.

followed this path. That rates of upward movement for sons listed in the same census as their fathers surpasses those for sons appearing ten years later, however, suggests that no direct relationship exists between rates of upward movement and the length of time elapsing in the comparison between fathers' and sons' occupation. In addition, movement into the white-collar group fluctuated over time and indicates neither an increase nor a decrease in upward mobility.

A slightly smaller proportion of blue-collar sons, ranging from 10 to 17 per cent depending on the type of father-son comparison made, entered the agricultural labor force. Most of these sons, like their white-collar counterparts, became farm operators rather than rural workers. In every type of comparison, the total number of sons becoming farm operators more than doubled the number entering the rural-workers group further indicating that those moving into an agricultural position tended to do so only after accumulating sufficient resources to become farm operators. However, the proportion both entering agricultural pursuits and becoming farm operators fell off sharply after 1870. Although the very small size of the sample necessitates caution regarding any conclusion, this does suggest that opportunity for blue-collar sons in the agricultural labor force declined after 1870. Lastly, combining rates of movement into both the white-collar and farm-operators group indicates that a substantial portion of these sons, ranging between 23 and 37 per cent, experienced occupational improvement, although the disproportionately high out-migration rates may inflate these rates by biasing the sample toward the most successful, i.e., sons of blue-collar workers who stayed in the community. Furthermore, these combined rates decline after 1870. Thus, similar to the patterns of intra-generational mobility for blue-collar workers, sons entering agriculture disproportionately tended to become farm operators and saw both their overall rates of movement and rates of occupational improvement decline over time.

Similar to the sons of white-collar workers, farm operators' sons also displayed low levels of occupational inheritance (see tables 38–40). In the three father-son sub-samples, the proportion retaining the same position as their fathers ranged between 40 and 60 per cent; more importantly the percentage

TABLE 38

INTER-GENERATIONAL MOBILITY PATTERNS FOR SONS (AGES 31–40) OF FARM
OPERATORS APPEARING IN THE SAME CENSUS AS THEIR FATHERS, 1850–1894

	1850	1860	1870	1880	Total* 1850–80	1894	
White-collar	0.0	0.0	6.7	16.7	11.4	100.0	0.0
Blue-collar	0.0	0.0	13.3	4.2	6.8	0.0	100.0
Farm Operators	0.0	66.7	66.7	29.2	43.2	0.0	0.0
Rural Workers	100.0	33.3	13.3	50.0	38.6	. .	. .
Sample	2	3	15	24	44	1	1

* For these and the following tables where the father's occupation was in agriculture, totals are based on sons' data to 1880 since available data for 1894 omit
agricultural workers and the census that year does not distinguish between farm
operators and rural workers.

becoming farm operators increased with time elapsing in the
comparison. This suggests that many farm operators' sons
pursued other occupations prior to ultimately taking over
their father's farm. However, that the proportion of sons
remaining farm operators fell over time, regardless of the
type of comparison made, indicates that opportunity in agriculture for these sons was diminishing.

For those sons leaving the farm-operators category, downward mobility into the rural-workers group predominated;
the total percentage following this path ranged between 17
and 39 per cent depending on the type of comparison. That
these rates fall as fathers' and sons' occupations are examined
at more comparable points in their careers strengthens the

TABLE 39

INTER-GENERATIONAL MOBILITY PATTERNS FOR SONS (AGES 31–40) OF FARM
OPERATORS APPEARING IN A CENSUS 10 YEARS LATER THAN THEIR FATHERS,
1850–1894

	Fathers 1850 Sons 1860	Fathers 1860 Sons 1870	Fathers 1870 Sons 1880	Total 1860–80	Fathers 1880 Sons 1894	
White-collar	0.0	0.0	16.7	11.5	14.3	36.4
Blue-collar	0.0	14.3	7.2	8.2	78.6	45.5
Farm Operators	60.0	71.4	50.0	55.7	7.1	18.2
Rural Workers	40.0	14.3	26.2	24.6	. .	. .
Sample	5	14	42	61	14	11

TABLE 40

INTER-GENERATIONAL MOBILITY PATTERNS FOR SONS (AGES 31–40) OF FARM
OPERATORS APPEARING IN A CENSUS 20 YEARS LATER THAN THEIR FATHERS,
1850–1894

	Fathers 1850 Sons 1870	Fathers 1860 Sons 1880	Total 1870–80	Fathers 1870	Sons 1894
White-collar	0.0	17.6	15.4	7.7	25.0
Blue-collar	0.0	11.8	10.3	76.9	58.3
Farm Operators	100.0	50.0	56.4	15.4	16.7
Rural Workers	0.0	20.6	17.9	. .	. .
Sample	5	34	39	13	12

contention that many of these sons were waiting to take over
their fathers' farms. However, the rates of downward movement tend to rise over time and particularly after 1870, further indicating both that the opportunity for these sons to
become farm operators was vanishing and that they most
fully account for the overall rise of inter-generational downward mobility in the community. Lastly, comparing patterns
of intra- and inter-generational movement suggests that farm
operators, like white-collar workers, found it easier to maintain their own positions than to pass them on to their sons.

In addition to falling into the rural-workers category, a
number of farmers' sons, ranging from 18 to 26 per cent
for the various sub-samples, entered the urban labor force.
Furthermore these proportions rose after 1870 reflecting
both the declining state of agriculture and the growing importance of non-agricultural activities in the community. Regardless of the type of comparison employed, moreover, the majority of these sons became white- rather than blue-collar
workers. This contrasts sharply with the pattern of intra-generational movement of farm operators who disproportionately entered blue-collar occupations and suggests that farm
operators' sons benefited more than farm operators by entering the urban labor force.

Mirroring rural workers patterns of intra-generational mobility, sons of rural workers exhibited the greatest amount
of movement of any group of sons; more than two-thirds
of the total in each of the sub-samples pursued occupations
different from their fathers' (see tables 41–43). These rates
also steadily increase over time for those enumerated in the

TABLE 41

INTER-GENERATIONAL MOBILITY PATTERNS FOR SONS (AGES 31–40) OF RURAL
WORKERS APPEARING IN THE SAME CENSUS AS THEIR FATHERS, 1850–1894

	1850	1860	1870	1880	Total 1850–80	1894	
White-collar	0.0	0.0	0.0	0.0	0.0	0.0	0.0
Blue-collar	0.0	0.0	12.5	33.3	11.5	0.0	0.0
Farm Operators	0.0	45.5	75.0	66.7	57.7	0.0	0.0
Rural Workers	100.0	54.5	12.5	0.0	30.8	. .	. .
Sample	1	11	8	6	26	0	0

same census as their fathers or listed in one ten years later indicating that rural workers' sons did not account for the overall decrease of inter-generational mobility in the community. However, that the pattern reversed itself for sons appearing twenty years later prohibits a firm conclusion regarding rural workers' sons mobility patterns.

Also comparable to patterns of intra-generational movement, rural workers' sons demonstrated a great deal of upward mobility; the total becoming farm operators exceeded 55 per cent for every comparison. Even more remarkable, a higher proportion of rural workers' offspring than farm operators' sons came to own their own farms. The extremely high out-migration rates of rural workers relative to farm operators (over three times greater), however, suggest that these inter-generational rates represent the success of an unrepresentative minority in contrast to those of farm operators' sons. Although these rates of upward movement are

TABLE 42

INTER-GENERATIONAL MOBILITY PATTERNS FOR SONS (AGES 31–40) OF RURAL
WORKERS APPEARING IN A CENSUS TEN YEARS LATER THAN THEIR FATHERS,
1850–1894

	Fathers 1850 Sons 1860	Fathers 1860 Sons 1870	Fathers 1870 Sons 1880	Total 1850–80	Fathers 1880 Sons 1894	
White-collar	0.0	17.6	25.0	13.3	0.0	0.0
Blue-collar	0.0	5.9	25.0	6.7	100.0	100.0
Farm Operators	55.5	70.6	50.0	63.3	0.0	0.0
Rural Workers	44.4	5.9	0.0	16.7	. .	. .
Sample	9	17	4	30	1	1

TABLE 43

INTER-GENERATIONAL MOBILITY PATTERNS FOR SONS (AGES 31–40) OF RURAL
WORKERS APPEARING IN A CENSUS TWENTY YEARS LATER THAN THEIR FATHERS,
1870–1894

	Fathers 1850 Sons 1870	Fathers 1860 Sons 1880	Total 1870–80	Fathers 1870 Sons 1894	
White-collar	7.1	7.1	7.1	0.0	50.0
Blue-collar	7.1	7.1	7.1	100.0	50.0
Farm Operators	71.4	57.1	64.3	0.0	0.0
Rural Workers	14.3	28.6	21.4	. .	. .
Sample	14	14	28	1	2

high, they fall in every sub-sample for sons after 1870. This not only reflects the declining opportunity in agriculture after the first two decades of settlement but also accounts most fully for the overall decline of inter-generational upward mobility in the community.

In addition to becoming farm operators, a small number, never more than 20 per cent of any of the sub-samples, entered the urban labor market. Those moving in this direction seem to have divided about equally into manual and non-manual workers. More specifically, a majority of the sons listed in the same census as their fathers became blue-collar workers while the reverse was true for those listed ten years later, and those enumerated twenty years later divided evenly between the two occupational categories. This also is in marked contrast to patterns of intra-generational mobility of rural workers which show that the vast majority became blue-collar workers. Thus rural workers' sons, like those of farm operators, appear to have been more successful than their fathers when taking up a non-agricultural occupation. Lastly, with the exception of the twenty-year father-son comparison, the proportion moving into urban occupations increased. This pattern coupled with decreasing upward mobility further implies that opportunity in agriculture declined over time for rural workers' sons.

IV.

Patterns and rates of inter-generational occupational mobility of sons in the thirty-one to forty age group mirrored trends in intra-generational movement. In general, gross rates of inter-generational mobility remained constant up to 1870. After this date, however, they declined but not to the extent revealed in the previous examination of intra-generational movement. Similarly, upward rates of inter-generational mobility showed the same dramatic decrease that intra-generational rates had after 1870. Also comparable to the earlier analysis, downward rates after an initial decrease rose markedly for sons after 1870. Thus, these trends indicate, just as intra-generational rates had, that the structural changes in the labor force stimulated by the settling and early development of the community provided a far greater impetus to occupational movement and opportunity than did the beginnings of urbanization and industrialization.

Patterns of gross, upward, and downward mobility of sons grouped according to their father's occupation both indicate that each group experienced substantial movement and offer further insights into overall patterns of inter-generational mobility. Both farm operators and white-collar workers had surprisingly high rates of downward mobility in contrast to much lower rates in the intra-generational examination. Furthermore, downward movement tended to occur with greater frequency in each successive time period for both groups. Similar to patterns found in the intra-generational study, rural workers' sons displayed extremely high rates of upward movement into the farm-operators category to the extent that a larger proportion of them became farm operators than did farm operators' sons. Part of the explanation for this development may be that the exceptionally high out-migration rates of rural workers severely skews the sample toward the most successful rural workers and their sons. Increased rural to urban and decreased upward inter-generational movement of these sons, however, reflected the growing lack of opportunity in the agricultural sector of the economy and help to account for the respective overall rise and fall in these types of mobility. Sons of blue-collar workers, by contrast, exhibited the least amount of inter-generational movement. Moreover, their gross rates of mobility declined and reflected the overall decrease in son's movement. Nevertheless, a substantial minority of these sons of blue-collar workers (23 to 37 per cent) entered either the white-collar or farm-operators group; no doubt, the disproportionately high out-migration rate of manual workers helps explain these high levels of mobility. Lastly, these combined rates of movement fell as time passed indicating that the opportunity for occupational improvement was diminishing just as both overall inter-generational patterns and the intra-generational rates for blue-collar workers had.

Movement from an urban to a rural and from a rural to an urban occupation, in contrast to the examination of intra-generational mobility, more clearly reflected the growing importance of the non-agricultural sector of the economy. That is, mobility from an urban to a rural category showed a definite decrease while movement in the opposite direction rose. In addition, patterns of inter-generational mobility of sons whose fathers were employed in agriculture reveal that a larger proportion became white-collar workers than did the patterns of intra-generational movement of agricultural workers who entered the urban labor force. On the other hand, sons of urban workers, similar to the intra-generational examination of urban workers, tended to become farm operators rather than rural workers upon entering agriculture.

VI. Patterns of Wealth Mobility in the Holland Community

Thus far the analysis has focused on an examination of both intra-generational and inter-generational occupational mobility. By inferring changes in wealth from changes in occupation, it is possible to offer some estimates of the degree and patterns of economic opportunity extant in the Holland community between 1850 and 1894. An alternative to the inferential method is to measure directly changes in the amount of wealth possessed by members of the community.

While the direct measurement of wealth mobility is no doubt preferable to the inferential method, a number of difficulties restrict the utility of the former approach. The greatest single obstacle to the direct measurement arises from the fact that only fragmentary data pertaining to wealth are available. As previously noted in Chapter IV, the tax records of the Holland community are organized in such a fashion as to make them useless for the study of economic mobility. These documents contain only the individual's name and the value of a particular tract of land as well as an estimation of his personal wealth. Unfortunately, persons owning more than one tract of land are often listed in more than one place throughout the reports thus making it difficult to obtain an accurate picture of the individual's total wealth. These lists, moreover, lack essential information about the persons enumerated to permit an appraisal of either intra-generational or inter-generational wealth mobility. Only the subject's name and wealth are provided; information necessary for identification and consequently for tracing individual career patterns or son's career such as age, wife's name, and the names and ages of children is omitted.

The manuscripts of the federal census offer more adequate sources of information bearing on this problem, although

omissions in these data limit their usefulness for an extensive
examination of wealth mobility. In 1860 and 1870 these reports list the wealth, both real and personal, of all members
of the community and the 1850 enumeration provides only
information on the real estate holdings of each resident. Unfortunately, the federal census of 1880 and the state census
of 1894 do not contain similarly valuable evidence. As a result
of these omissions, the analysis of intra-generational wealth
mobility is confined to the period between 1850 and 1870;
such restrictions prohibit an investigation of long-range
trends in economic mobility.

The fragmentary nature of the data, perhaps even more
importantly, precludes any meaningful examination of inter-
generational wealth mobility. Given the extent of the information available, it is only possible to compare father's wealth
with that of his son twenty years later at one point, father's
wealth in 1850 and son's in 1870. Similarly, comparing father's and son's wealth at points ten years apart offers only
two points of observation, father's wealth in 1850 and 1860
with son's in 1860 and 1870. Consequently, that the two
most important types of observations for examining inter-
generational mobility are severely restricted clearly indicates
that an appraisal of inter-generational wealth mobility is not
profitable.

The manuscripts of the federal censuses contain other
weaknesses that raise questions about their reliability. It is
reasonable to assume that they possess a number of inaccuracies regarding the amount of wealth attributed to each resident. The estimation of personal wealth, based on both tangible and intangible assets, immediately lends itself to
distortion. A second point challenging the veracity of these
records is that no mention is made as to whether the person
owned the property outright or whether there was a large
mortgage on the land, an important consideration in estimat-
ing an individual's wealth. That the census-taker did not always report property values of less than $50 further weakens
the value of these documents. Such discretion no doubt had
a profound effect upon the 1850 census of the Holland community because during the first three years of settlement
town lots initially sold for $10 to $15 each with the price
later being raised to $38 for lots in the middle of the block

and $48 for corner lots.[1] Consequently, for many people in a newly settled community like Holland, ownership of property might not be recorded by the census taker. Thus, while the limited nature of the information contained in the manuscripts of the federal census restricts the scope of the study of wealth mobility, errors and important omissions in the data themselves further necessitate that conclusions drawn from the manuscripts be qualified.

Not only does the lack of sound data hinder the study of wealth mobility, but also the measurement of such movement presents problems, although methodological considerations do not appear to be commensurate with those involving occupational mobility. Even though a hierarchy of wealth obviously exists and is easily detectable, a problem arises in establishing meaningful wealth intervals. Such a decision is of extreme importance since the setting of these intervals, an arbitrary decision, can bias the data and profoundly alter the results of any examination of wealth mobility. For example, if the intervals are set extremely high, it would not be surprising to find extremely low rates of movement. To illustrate this point let us assume that we have a sample in which 2 per cent of the group possesses wealth in excess of $5,000 and the remainder consists of persons each with accumulations totaling less than $1,000. Setting the wealth intervals $5,000 apart means that for the overwhelming majority of the sample to display movement they would have to improve their financial position by over $4,000, a rather rigid requirement given the distribution of wealth in the sample. On the other hand, if the wealth intervals for the above group were made substantially smaller, the opposite effect would be achieved. Thus, setting intervals of $100 for the above distribution would greatly inflate rates of wealth mobility; that is, in order to display movement one at the most would only have to increase his stock of wealth by $100 rather than by $4,000 as in the previous example.

The main difficulty in setting up wealth intervals is that the wealth hierarchy of the Holland settlement became more highly differentiated between 1850 and 1870. This point is illustrated by the fact that only one person enumerated in

---

[1] Lucas, 1955: p. 96.

both the censuses of 1850 and 1860 possessed real wealth in 1850 in excess of $2,000 and, by 1860, 14.4 per cent of the sample had total wealth equal to more than $2,000. Moreover, of those in the 1850 census who remained in the community until 1870, 58.8 per cent had more than $2,000 in property and personal wealth whereas in 1850 only one person fell into this category. Similarly, those who appeared in both the censuses of 1860 and 1870 indicated a substantial movement toward a more highly differentiated distribution of wealth. In 1860 only 8.8 per cent possessed wealth valued at more than $2,000. However, ten years later this proportion had increased dramatically to 53.3 per cent of the labor force.

From this general description of the changes in the amount of wealth possessed by the residents of the Holland community, it becomes apparent that no set of perfect wealth categories can be established. Taking into consideration these difficulties, I have established four wealth categories of $0–$1,000, $1,001–$2,000, $2,001–$3,000, and $3,001 and above for this study. While in large part this is an arbitrary classification, it does have some virtues given the distribution of wealth in the Holland community between 1850 and 1870. Thus, four wealth intervals of $1,000 each were decided upon because this would give the best possible set of intervals. Moreover, when these distinctions are applied to the data on total wealth for 1870 which is the final year in the analysis, a reasonably equal distribution of wealth is achieved with no fewer than 17 per cent of the sample falling into each category whether it be for the group composed of those appearing in both the censuses of 1850 and 1870 or 1860 and 1870. However, obvious weaknesses to these divisions do exist. When applied to the wealth data for 1850, they elicit a highly skewed distribution with over 98 per cent of the sample falling into the smallest wealth category. Lowering the first wealth interval from $1,000 to $250 would only reduce the proportion falling into the first category to slightly under 80 per cent of the total sample. In addition, setting the figure this low would greatly inflate upward rates of wealth mobility. This clustering of people at the bottom of the wealth hierarchy is not surprising in a newly established community with substantial numbers of new arrivals each day; one would not expect to find many people in possession of large tracts of improved land for the clearing and cultivation of land takes time.

Other problems, in addition to setting wealth intervals, need to be dealt with before examining economic mobility. As previously noted, data for 1850 consist of information pertaining only to real estate holdings, while for 1860 and 1870 records on both personal and real assets are available. The problem then becomes: should only the value of real estate holdings for all censuses be used or should real wealth in 1850 be compared with figures for total wealth in 1860 and 1870? The latter option was chosen for a number of reasons. In 1850, three years after the settlement of the colony, the value of real estate holdings offers a good indication of an individual's total wealth since the majority of the residents were either involved in agriculture or immediately concerned with the task of obtaining and clearing land. In addition, there is little reason to suspect that many members of the community possessed large amounts of personal wealth; the memoirs of the early settlers of the community are in total agreement that wealth in the early days of the community was limited to a "few crude tools."[2] However, with the economic development of the community, real wealth becomes less valuable as an indicator of total wealth. As the proportion of people employed in non-agricultural occupations rose, it seems reasonable to assume that personal wealth became increasingly important to a sizable portion of the population.[3] Data on personal wealth from the censuses of 1860 and 1870 offer support for this assumption. The proportion of people listed in each enumeration with $250 or less personal wealth fell from 80.7 per cent in 1860 to 56.7 per cent in 1870. By contrast, the proportion with more than $2,500 rose from 0.5 per cent to 2.4 per cent and the percentage having more than $1,000 almost doubled, 3.3 per cent in 1860 as opposed to 6.3 per cent in 1870. Therefore, given the nature of the data and the community's development, it appears that the most accurate means of measuring wealth mobility is to use real wealth for 1850 and total wealth for 1860 and 1870.

---

[2] See Lucas, 1955: *passim.*

[3] One would assume that businessmen and merchants would have a smaller portion of their wealth tied up in real estate than would farmers.

Other difficulties also permeate the study of wealth mobility in the late nineteenth century. While age is an important factor in occupational attainment and movement, it probably merits even more concern in an analysis of wealth mobility. It seems reasonable to assume that an individual reaches the peak of his occupational career at a far earlier age in life than he attains the height of his accumulation of wealth. To illustrate this point, one in general would assume that a lawyer at age thirty would possess a smaller fortune than a lawyer at age sixty. Thus, it appears that it is far more important to control for age in measuring wealth mobility than it is in measuring occupational movement. However, this assumption will be tested later in this chapter.

Not only is age an important consideration in the study of wealth mobility, but also to some extent one has to be aware of the influences of inflation; a society experiencing hyper-inflation, for example, would reveal high rates of mobility due to inflated prices rather than to any substantial changes in actual wealth. This problem, moreover, would appear to be particularly acute in a community like the Holland settlement between 1850 and 1870.[4] In a new community with an increasing population one would not be particularly shocked to find the price of land increasing dramatically from decade to decade. This plus the limited data pertaining to wealth would suggest that the results of any study need to be subjected to a number of qualifications. Nevertheless,

---

[4] Data on the rate of inflation and its effect on land values is rather sketchy for the Holland community. National data indicate that the per acre value of land increased more rapidly between 1850 and 1860 than it did between 1860 and 1870; the average value per acre of land was $11.14, $16.32, and $18.26 in 1850, 1860, and 1870 respectively. Information bearing on land values for Ottawa County, site of the Holland community, suggests a reversal of this pattern with a larger increase taking place in the 1860's than during the 1850's. The agricultural census of 1850 reported 4,904 acres of improved land and 19,054 acres of unimproved land valued at $191,297 in the county. The following census reported a substantial increase in all these figures listing 37,574 improved acres and 66,296 unimproved acres valued at $1,724,415. These figures suggest that there was a modest increase in the value of farm land during the 1850's in Ottawa County. Data for 1870 suggest that more substantial increases in the value of land took place in the 1860's than the 1850's. The agricultural census of 1870 reported 81,702 and 117,499 acres of improved and unimproved land respectively valued at $7,568,445. From this information, it appears that the greatest increase in land values in the Holland community occurred during the 1860's rather than the 1850's, thus running contrary to the national pattern.

such an analysis is necessary in order to have some idea of the relationship between occupational and wealth mobility in an emerging ethnic community.

Once it has been decided what wealth data to employ and what intervals to establish, it is then possible to proceed with the examination of economic movement. For this analysis, rates of wealth mobility will be calculated for the entire population and also for age groups. In addition to age, ethnicity will also be taken into consideration. The findings from these various appraisals will then be compared with the results from the earlier examination of intra-generational occupational mobility.

Summary measures of wealth mobility without controlling for any variables strongly indicate on the surface that economic mobility in some respects differed from occupational movement. The most striking fact is that substantial and increasing rates of economic movement, primarily upward, occurred in the Holland community between 1850 and 1870 (see table 44). Of those enumerated in both the censuses of 1850 and 1860, 41.0 per cent moved from one wealth category to another, and, with the exception of less than 1 per cent of the population, this mobility was upward. For those listed in the 1850 census who remained in the settlement until 1870, movement from one wealth category to another rose substantially; of those mobile, moreover, 66.5

TABLE 44

SUMMARY MEASURES OF INTRA-GENERATIONAL WEALTH MOBILITY BASED ON DATA FROM THE CENSUSES OF 1850, 1860, and 1870

	1850 Real Wealth and 1860 Total Wealth	1850 Real Wealth and 1870 Total Wealth	1860 Total Wealth and 1870 Total Wealth
Percentage Mobile	41.9	69.0	77.0
Percentage Upwardly Mobile	41.3	66.5	76.0
Percentage Downwardly Mobile	0.6	2.5	1.0
Sample	332	304	658

per cent moved upward and only 2.5 per cent saw their economic position decline. The rate of economic movement for those enumerated in both the censuses of 1860 and 1870 far surpassed that for those listed in both the 1850 and 1860 censuses. Of the former group, over three-fourths experienced mobility with all but 1 per cent improving their position.

These patterns differ in many respects from those of intragenerational occupational mobility. The most significant departure is that rates of occupational movement revealed a steady decline whereas rates of wealth mobility substantially increased. In absolute terms, the two rates reversed themselves. From the 1850–1860 period, the rate of occupational mobility employing four occupational categories was higher than the rate of economic movement, 64.7 per cent as opposed to 41.9 per cent. On the other hand, during the following decade the rate of wealth mobility far exceeded that of occupational movement with 77.0 per cent experiencing the former and only 39.6 per cent the latter. Although gross rates of movement between the two types of mobility varied in the two decades under consideration, upward wealth mobility was always larger and tended to increase while upward occupational movement was smaller and tended to decrease.

Even though a number of important differences existed between the two different types of movement, the chances for both types of movement greatly increased with the length of time spent in the community. For those who appeared in both the censuses of 1850 and 1870, rates of occupational and wealth mobility were far higher than for those enumerated in the censuses of 1850 and 1860. However, even here a major difference exists. The differential in rate of movement between those enumerated in the 1850 and 1870 census and those listed in 1850 and 1860 is greater for wealth mobility than it is for occupational movement, the differential being 26.9 per cent for the former and 12.1 per cent for the latter.

While in many respects little relationship seems to exist between occupational and wealth mobility, a closer inspection of the wealth mobility tables constructed for those appearing in the three censuses under consideration suggests just the opposite (see tables 45–47). As previously noted the most striking feature of these charts is that over 98 per cent and

TABLE 45

Rates of Intra-generational Wealth Mobility, Real Wealth in 1850 versus Total Wealth in 1860

	Under $1,000	$1,001– 2,000	$2,001– 3,000	$3,001– and Above	Total
Under $1,001	192[1] 58.4[2] 99.0[3] 57.8[4]	89 27.3 98.4 26.8	26 8.0 96.3 7.8	19 5.8 90.5 5.7	326 100.0 98.2 98.2
$1,001– 2,000	2 40.0 1.0 0.6	1 20.0 1.1 0.3	1 20.0 3.7 0.3	1 20.0 4.8 0.3	5 100.0 1.5 1.5
$2,001– 3,000	0 0.0 0.0 0.0	0 0.0 0.0 0.0	0 0.0 0.0 0.0	1 100.0 4.8 0.3	1 100.0 0.3 0.3
$3,001– and Above	0 0.0 0.0 0.0	0 0.0 0.0 0.0	0 0.0 0.0 0.0	0 0.0 0.0 0.0	0 0.0 0.0 0.0
Total	194 100.0 58.4	90 100.0 27.1	27 100.0 8.1	21 100.0 6.3	332 100.0 100.0

[1] Figures in upper left-hand corner represent the absolute number in the sample.
[2] Figures in lower left-hand corner represent percentage of column total.
[3] Figures in upper right-hand corner represent percentage of row total.
[4] Figures in lower right-hand corner represent percentage of total sample.

TABLE 46

Rates of Intra-generational Wealth Mobility, Real Wealth in 1850 versus Total Wealth in 1870

	Under $1,001		$1,001–2,000		$2,001–3,000		$3,001– and Above		Total	
Under $1,001	70[1] 23.5[2]	95.9[3] 23.0[4]	52 17.4	100.0 17.1	52 17.4	98.1 17.1	124 41.6	98.4 40.8	298 100.0	98.0 98.0
$1,001– 2,000	3 50.0	4.1 1.0	0 0.0	0 0.0	1 16.7	1.9 0.3	2 33.3	1.6 0.7	6 100.0	2.0 2.0
$2,001– 3,000	0 0.0	0 0.0	0 0.0	0 0.0	0 0.0	0.0 0.0	0 0.0	0.0 0.0	0 0.0	0.0 0.0
$3,001– and Above	0 0.0	0 0.0	0 0.0	0 0.0	0 0.0	0.0 0.0	0 0.0	0.0 0.0	0 0.0	0.0 0.0
Total	73 24.0	100.0 100.0	52 17.1	100.0 100.0	53 17.4	100.0 100.0	126 41.4	100.0 100.0	304 100.0	100.0 100.0

[1] Figures in upper left-hand corner represent the absolute number in the sample.
[2] Figures in lower left-hand corner represent percentage of column total.
[3] Figures in upper right-hand corner represent percentage of row total.
[4] Figures in lower right-hand corner represent percentage of total sample.

TABLE 47

RATES OF INTRA-GENERATIONAL WEALTH MOBILITY, TOTAL WEALTH IN 1860 VERSUS TOTAL WEALTH IN 1870

Each cell shows four figures: upper-left = absolute number; upper-right = % of row total; lower-left = % of column total; lower-right = % of total sample.

	Under $1,001	$1,001–2,000	$2,001–3,000	$3,001–and Above	Total
Under $1,001	167[1] 35.9[3] 91.3[2] 25.4[4]	113 24.3 91.1 17.2	86 18.5 69.4 13.1	99 21.3 43.6 15.0	465 100.0 70.7 70.7
$1,001–2,000	14 10.4 7.7 2.1	11 8.1 8.9 1.7	30 22.2 24.2 4.6	80 59.3 35.2 12.2	135 100.0 20.5 20.5
$2,001–3,000	2 5.6 1.1 0.3	0 0.0 0.0 0.0	6 16.7 4.8 0.9	28 77.8 12.3 4.3	36 100.0 5.5 5.5
$3,001–and Above	0 0.0 0.0 0.0	0 0.0 0.0 0.0	2 9.1 1.6 0.3	20 90.0 8.8 3.0	22 100.0 3.3 3.3
Total	183 27.8 100.0 27.8	124 18.8 100.0 18.8	124 18.8 100.0 18.8	227 34.5 100.0 34.5	658 100.0 100.0 100.0

[1] Figures in upper left-hand corner represent the absolute number in the sample.
[2] Figures in lower left-hand corner represent percentage of column total.
[3] Figures in upper right-hand corner represent percentage of row total.
[4] Figures in lower right-hand corner represent percentage of total sample.

70 per cent respectively of those enumerated in the censuses of 1850 and 1860 fall into the first wealth category under $1,000. The overwhelming majority of those listed in both 1850 and 1860, however, did have real estate listed in the 1850 enumeration. In addition none of this land or only a small portion of it had been improved. Within the next ten years substantial portions were cleared and this combined with the increasing population of the Holland community no doubt resulted in rising land values thereby stimulating high rates of upward wealth mobility. An acceleration of these processes during the 1860's combined with a more general nationwide increase in land values offers a strong explanation of why wealth mobility rates climbed between 1860 and 1870.

A review of the data on occupational mobility further explains why changes in economic mobility are not reflected in rates of occupational movement. Between 1850 and 1860 almost three-fourths of the occupational movement was into the farm-operators category, 47.2 per cent of the entire population (64.4 per cent had been mobile). Thus what appears to have taken place during the 1850's is that the movement into the farm-operators category as a result of clearing land reflected the increase in land values. Between 1860 and 1870, with a much higher proportion of the population already in the farm-operators category and consequently a smaller percentage, 25.6 per cent as opposed to 47.2 per cent, entering the farm-operators category, occupational mobility declined and consequently did not mirror the continuing increase in land values. Instead, the continuing increase in land values was reflected not in movement between the broad occupational groups but by movement within the farm-operators category. Almost two-thirds of the farm operators became proprietors of substantially larger farms.[5] Consequently, if these factors are taken into consideration, it appears that wealth mobility may indeed have come closer to approximating rates of occupational movement than the various summary measures indicate.

These results, furthermore, do not dispute the findings from the study of occupational mobility which indicated that economic mobility declined after 1870. Data on movement

---

[5] See Chapter IV.

into the farm-operators group and mobility within this group strongly suggest that economic movement declined. By the 1870's, the proportion of the population moving into the farm-operators category had slipped to 4.8 per cent compared with 25.6 per cent the previous decade. In addition, upward mobility within the farm-operators group to more prosperous farms declined from 65.8 per cent in the 1860's to 26.7 per cent during the 1870's.

When rates of intra-generational wealth mobility are examined controlling for age, the greatest rates of movement take place in older age groups than they did for a similar analysis of occupational mobility (see tables 48–50). Of those who appeared in both the censuses of 1850 and 1860, the highest rates of economic movement occur among those in the twenty-one to thirty and thirty-one to forty age groups with over 45 per cent in each cohort displaying movement. Similarly the highest rates of wealth mobility for those appearing in both the censuses of 1850 and 1870 occur among those in the twenty-one to thirty and thirty-one to forty age brackets with over 85 per cent of both groups being mobile. By contrast, individuals in the thirty-one to forty and forty-one to fifty age groups of those appearing in both the censuses of 1860 and 1870 reported the highest rates of wealth mobility with over three-fourths experiencing movement. One possible explanation of this shift toward older cohorts might well be that in the early years of settlement, up to about 1855, people between the ages of twenty-one and forty were best

TABLE 48

RATES OF INTRA-GENERATIONAL WEALTH MOBILITY FOR THOSE APPEARING IN BOTH THE CENSUSES OF 1850 AND 1860, CONTROLLING FOR AGE IN 1850

	Under 20	21–30	31–40	41–50	51–60
Percentage Mobile	29.2	51.3	46.2	38.3	26.7
Percentage Upwardly Mobile	29.2	51.3	46.2	36.9	23.4
Percentage Downwardly Mobile	0.0	0.0	0.0	1.4	3.3
Sample	24	76	117	73	30

TABLE 49

RATES OF INTRA-GENERATIONAL WEALTH MOBILITY FOR THOSE APPEARING IN BOTH
THE CENSUSES OF 1860 AND 1870, CONTROLLING FOR AGE IN 1860

	Under 20	21–30	31–40	41–50	51–60
Percentage Mobile	43.3	68.7	80.9	78.5	66.7
Percentage Upwardly Mobile	41.9	68.0	79.7	77.3	56.4
Percentage Downwardly Mobile	1.5	0.7	1.2	1.2	10.3
Sample	67	134	173	163	78

equipped to take advantage of opportunities in a newly settled community. By the time of the enumeration of the population in 1860, most of these individuals would then fall into
either the thirty-one to forty or forty-one to fifty age groups.
Such an explanation would account for differences in mobility
rates among various age cohorts for the 1850's and 1860's.

Rates of wealth mobility follow a different pattern from
rates of occupational movement for various age cohorts. As
the examination of intra-generational occupational mobility
in Chapter IV revealed, the highest rates of movement took
place among those in the twenty-one to thirty and under
twenty age groups. By contrast, this analysis of wealth mobility indicates that the highest rates took place among those
in the twenty-one to thirty and thirty-one to forty age brackets

TABLE 50

RATES OF INTRA-GENERATIONAL WEALTH MOBILITY FOR THOSE APPEARING IN BOTH
THE CENSUSES OF 1850 AND 1870, CONTROLLING FOR AGE IN 1850

	Under 20	21–30	31–40	41–50	51–60
Percentage Mobile	72.0	89.3	86.5	70.1	40.9
Percentage Upwardly Mobile	72.0	89.3	86.5	67.1	36.4
Percentage Downwardly Mobile	0.0	0.0	0.0	3.0	4.5
Sample	25	75	104	67	22

TABLE 51

RATES OF INTRA-GENERATIONAL WEALTH MOBILITY OF DUTCH-BORN AND NON-DUTCH-
BORN, 1860–1870

	Dutch Born	Non-Dutch Born
Percentage Mobile	70.5	48.9
Percentage Upwardly Mobile	68.2	44.6
Percentage Downwardly Mobile	2.3	4.3
Sample	611	47

of all those listed in the census of 1850 and within the thirty-one to forty and forty-one to fifty age groups for those enumerated in 1860. Such findings tend to confirm the hypothesis that higher occupational status is achieved at an earlier age than higher wealth status.

Controlling for ethnicity proves to be an important factor in determining rates of wealth mobility. The data for those settlers who appeared in both the censuses of 1860 and 1870 strongly indicate that the Dutch-born majority experienced much higher rates of movement than did the non-Dutch residents (see table 51).[6] Rates of wealth mobility for the Dutch-born population exceed 70 per cent while those for the non-Dutch segment are just under 50 per cent. By contrast, rates of downward mobility for non-Dutch residents exceed those for the Dutch-born population, 4.3 versus 2.3 per cent. One possible explanation for this difference is that twice as many (64 versus 30 per cent) of the Dutch-born as non-Dutch-born listed in both the 1860 and 1870 censuses were farm operators in 1870, an occupational group that might well experience greater wealth mobility given the rising value of land in the first two decades of the community's development.

The results of this examination of wealth mobility in the Holland community do not differ substantially from those of occupational mobility. While on the surface it appears that substantial differences existed between occupational and wealth mobility rates, a closer inspection reveals that this was due to increased land values resulting largely from the

---

[6] The data for 1850 were not used because there were only seven non-Dutch adult males in the community.

clearing of land in a newly settled community. However, this was a temporary phenomenon which does not dispute the conclusion that mobility in general declined after 1870 in the Holland community. When the factor of age was considered, it is found that the highest rates of movement took place among slightly older age groups than did the highest rates of occupational mobility. The introduction of the factor of ethnicity into the appraisal of economic mobility revealed that unlike occupational movement, the Dutch-born majority enjoyed far greater opportunity for advancement than did the non-Dutch minority.

VII. Conclusions

I.

THIS ANALYSIS of social and geographic mobility has focused on nineteenth-century Holland, Michigan, a community comparable in size and ethnic homogeneity to many other settlements yet distinct from those communities in which mobility has been previously examined. In contrast to other areas studied, Holland possessed an ethnically homogeneous population similar to a large number of ethnic enclaves dotting the Middle West. In addition, the important role of agriculture in its economic life contrasts sharply with both the medium-sized and the large cities previously examined. Moreover, the growing importance of light industry serves also to differentiate it from Trempealeau County. Thus, the Holland community represents a fourth type of community needed to be studied in order to understand more fully the mobility process in nineteenth-century America.

During the years of this study, the Holland community experienced substantial changes in both its population and economic life. Not only did the population increase more than five-fold in these years but also concentrated population centers arose. In addition, improvements in water transportation and the coming of the railroad had by 1870 tied the community's economy to both regional and national markets. Partly as a result of these transportation improvements, gains to both the agricultural and industrial sectors of the economy far outstripped increases in population. The most spectacular of these advances accrued to the industrial sector which expanded at a rate fifteen times faster than the population. Similarly the agricultural sector also displayed tremendous growth in the first two decades of settlement; after 1870, however, it grew at a much slower rate as light export industry played an increasingly predominant role in the economy.

The impact of these economic developments produced major alterations in the size and composition of the labor force
as the number of employed males jumped almost four-fold
to slightly more than 2,000 between 1850 and 1880. Both
relatively and absolutely, the non-agricultural labor force
showed substantial gains among both white- and blue-collar
workers. Moreover, with the emergence of the factory semi-
skilled workers recorded the largest relative increases among
the latter. In addition these years also witnessed a decline
of almost 20 per cent in the proportion directly involved
in agriculture although the proportion of farm operators and
the percentage possessing more valuable farms increased
dramatically.

A number of demographic factors accounted for both increases and changes in the size and composition of the community's labor force. The net gain of 1,500 to the work force
involved a turnover of more than 4,000 people. Contributing
over 85 per cent of the total gains, the differential between
in- and out-migration also supplied all the increases to the
labor force and offset deficits resulting from net-natural processes in the first two decades of settlement. With the maturing
of the community in the 1870's, however, net-natural processes came to play a more positive role than before in expanding the labor force while net-migration, although continuing
to be the largest source of increase, assumed a relatively
less important role.

Among occupational groups there was a tendency for net-
migration to supply a larger proportion of increases to lower
than higher income positions. Within the urban sector, net-
migration contributed a greater proportion of increases to
blue- than to white-collar positions while the two internal
processes, net-natural forces and net-occupational mobility,
combined supplied larger gains to white- than to blue-collar
positions. Similarly within the agricultural occupational structure, net-migration tended to supply a disproportionately
larger increase or smaller decrease to the economically less
prestigious occupations. Lastly, the analysis of the relative
roles of net-migration and net-occupational mobility in altering the occupational structure challenges Goldstein's contention that the two complement each other in meeting a community's occupational needs and suggests that his model

underestimates the complexity of the relationship between vertical and horizontal movement and ignores the role of net-natural processes.

The analyses of in- and out-migration and the other components of change on the composition of the labor force also offer insights into nineteenth-century society that have broader implications for the study of social mobility. Although out-migration rates in the Holland community were lower in the first two decades of its settlement than those of other newly established rural communities, these rates, similar to the findings for other urban and rural nineteenth-century communities, were highest for those at the bottom of the occupational hierarchy. In addition, in-migration rates even more closely followed this pattern. The tendency of lower occupational groups in the Holland community to have higher rates of in- and out-migration, of net-migration to supply disproportionate increases to less prosperous occupations while internal processes disporportionately increased the more prosperous groups, and of opportunity for gross and upward mobility to increase with length of residency in the settlement implies that vertical movement was more likely to occur to those remaining in a settlement than to those geographically mobile. That is, the nineteenth-century man on the move, unlike his twentieth-century counterpart, was not the successful man on the make.

These results also suggest that studies of occupational mobility in any nineteenth-century community are dealing with an unrepresentative sample skewed toward the most occupationally mobile. In addition, the lack of a positive relationship between geographic mobility and upward vertical mobility in the nineteenth century and the contrary findings of Blau and Duncan for the twentieth century emphasize the need to incorporate systematically these factors into historical studies of other social and political phenomena.[1] In particular, future research should focus on the effect of the differing patterns of migration and its possible effects on family structure and behavior between classes over time. These migration patterns may also be important variables in understanding both the nature and social control of dissent and discontent.

---

[1] Blau and Duncan, 1967: pp. 243–275.

Finally, the apparent differences in these two relationships over time indicate that an assessment of the influence of migration should be incorporated in both spatial and temporal studies of community power and political power in general.

The examination of intra-generational occupational mobility, which was used as an indicator of economic mobility, reveals that residents of the community experienced substantial movement. This mobility, however, was not equally distributed over time. Somewhat suggestive of the Turner thesis regarding the level of opportunity available on the frontier, the pattern of movement in the settlement indicates that occupational mobility declined and the occupational structure became more rigid with the passage of time. Regardless of the type of occupational classification employed, gross mobility displayed a significant decrease particularly after 1870 and the strength of the association between beginning and ending occupation became increasingly stronger in later decades. Moreover, these changes were most pronounced when four broad occupational categories, which provide the best indicator of significant mobility, are employed. Not only did gross rates of movement decline but also rates of upward mobility fell at an even more rapid rate while significant increases characterized rates of downward movement after 1870 resulting in both mobility and the opportunity for economic advancement becoming less common after the initial decades of settlement.

Decreasing rates of change in the community's occupational structure offer the best explanation for these changing rates of movement; both minimum structural movement and structural changes based on the entire labor force fell substantially after 1870. This decline in structural change reduced the rate of increase in the number of new positions at the top and consequently curtailed the opportunity for those at the bottom of the occupational ladder to move upward while increasing the likelihood that those at the top would experience downward mobility. Thus, the structural changes accompanying the settlement and early development of the community offered greater inducements to mobility than did those changes brought about by urbanization and industrialization. Such findings raise doubts about the Lipset and Bendix thesis that social mobility increases concomitantly with industrialization, urbanization, and bureaucratization.[2] On the other hand, circulation or the mutual exchange of occupations tended to increase suggesting that a dynamic reverse correlation may exist between circulation and the amount of structural change occurring.

Examining the mobility rates of the various occupational categories in the Holland community reveals that those at the bottom of the occupational structure experienced the highest rates of movement. Only in one decade did fewer than two-thirds of the rural workers become farm operators while only in the last time period did fewer than one-third of the blue-collar workers enter either the white-collar or farm-operators category. In part these high rates can be explained by the disproportionately high out-migration rates of these less economically prestigious groups which serve to skew the sample toward the most successful. Nevertheless, these rates were impressive and, coupled with the high rates of economic improvement displayed by those whose occupational careers could be traced back to The Netherlands, indicate that the newly settled Holland community offered substantial opportunity for advancement. Thus, although many did not enjoy upward vertical movement and a large number left the community without achieving success, a sufficient number of cases of mobility probably existed to allow a substantial proportion of the population to believe that the American dream was within their grasp. This may have been especially true in a community composed of immigrants from a country they felt to be socially and economically stagnant.

Although those at the bottom experienced the highest rates of mobility, these groups also saw their rates of movement fall the fastest when the occupational structure tightened. The initial decline in the 1870's can be directly attributed to the decreasing rates of movement by rural workers. That fewer farm operators entered more affluent rankings within their broad group also indicates that declining opportunity in the agricultural sector accompanied urbanization and industrialization in the Holland community. Moreover, falling blue-collar rates of movement after 1880 sustained this pat-

---

[2] Lipset and Bendix, 1967: *passim*.

tern of declining mobility while white-collar rates after 1870 most fully account for the increase in downward movement after 1870. These patterns further demonstrate that the movement away from an agricultural-based economy did not offer the same opportunities for advancement as the settlement and early development of the community did.

Rural to urban occupational mobility, which represents one conception of urbanization, and urban to rural movement further indicate that the process of urbanization did not directly offer greater opportunity for upward mobility. Although the vast majority of those in the non-agricultural labor force became farm operators upon entering the agricultural labor force, less than half of those employed in agriculture became white-collar workers upon entering the non-agricultural labor market. Similarly the proportion of sons of fathers holding non-agricultural positions becoming farm operators upon entering agriculture surpassed the percentage of agricultural employees' sons becoming white-collar workers when entering the non-agricultural labor force.

Overall patterns and rates of inter-generational movement also mirrored trends in intra-generational occupational movement. Gross rates of inter-generational occupational mobility remained constant up to 1870, but after this date they declined somewhat although not to the extent that rates of intra-generational mobility had. Likewise, rates of upward inter-generational mobility tended to decline with the approach of the twentieth century, particularly after 1870. On the other hand, downward rates of movement increased markedly after 1870.

Patterns of inter-generational mobility of sons grouped according to their father's occupation indicate that each group experienced high rates of mobility. More specifically sons of white-collar workers and farm operators had higher rates of downward movement than did white-collar workers and farm operators in the analysis of intra-generational mobility. Sons of rural workers, similar to the pattern of intra-generational movement of rural workers, demonstrated a great deal of upward mobility. Likewise, blue-collar sons, although the least mobile group, still saw a large percentage of their number enter either white-collar or farm-operator positions. The high level of upward movement of sons of blue-collar workers, as in the case of intra-generational mobility, can be partly explained by the disproportionately high out-migration rates of those at the bottom of the occupational hierarchy. That downward movement for sons of white-collar workers and farm operators exceeded intra-generational rates for these occupational groups further indicates that it was easier for an individual holding a high-status occupation to maintain it for himself than to pass it on to his son.

The results of the analysis of intra-generational wealth mobility do not vary substantially from the examination of occupational movement. While at first glance major differences seem to exist between rates of wealth and occupational mobility, a closer inspection reveals that this was due to rapidly increasing land values resulting largely from the clearing of land in a newly settled community. This, however, was a temporary phenomenon that does not dispute the conclusion that mobility in general declined after 1870 in the Holland community.

Controlling for the factors of age and ethnicity reveals some differences between occupational and wealth mobility. The introduction of the factor of ethnicity into the appraisal of wealth mobility indicates that, unlike occupational movement, the Dutch-born majority enjoyed far greater opportunity for advancement than did the non-Dutch-born minority. Similarly a consideration of the factor of age shows that the highest rates of movement took place among slightly older age groups than did the highest rates of occupational mobility.

II.

By comparing these findings with those from other studies of mobility, it is possible to evaluate more fully the degree and pattern of mobility in the Holland community particularly in the first two decades of its settlement, the amount of opportunity available to those at the bottom of the occupational structure, and the influence of structural changes on the mobility process over time and space. The first part of this examination consists of comparing rates of intra-generational movement in the Holland community with those for eight other nineteenth- and twentieth-century communities which, with the exception of Trempealeau County, all represent either medium-sized or large urban areas. Consequently occupational mobility in these urban areas will be measured by the proportion of individuals crossing the blue-collar/white-collar line. On the other hand, because both the Holland community and Trempealeau County possessed large numbers of people employed in agriculture three different measures of occupational mobility will be employed in order to make thorough comparisons of communities possessing different occupational structures. The first measure of mobility will include among the mobile all those moving between four broad occupational categories—white-collar, blue-collar, farm-operator, and rural-worker. The second measure will exclude those moving across the agricultural/non-agricultural line from the mobility matrix and count among the occupationally mobile only those moving upward or downward within the urban and rural occupational hierarchies. The final measure will include in the mobility matrix only those remaining within the urban occupational structure.

The most striking difference in comparing mobility rates in Holland with those from other studies is that gross rates of movement in the first two decades of settlement were substantially higher than any of those for urban areas or for Holland after 1870 (see table 52). In these two time periods gross mobility totaled 64.7 and 39.6 per cent respectively when all types of movement are considered and 49.6 and 31.2 per cent when those moving across the agricultural/non-agricultural line are excluded from the mobility matrix. Only Trempealeau County with rates of both 43.5 and 38.2 and 32.6 and 31.3 for the respective measures of gross mobility in the first two decades of its settlement approaches those for Holland. In contrast, gross mobility never exceeded 18 per cent in any of the cities, and in Holland in the two time periods after 1870 it hovered around 20 per cent when all types of movement are considered and around 13 per cent when those moving across the urban/rural line are excluded from the mobility matrix. Comparing mobility rates for only those remaining within the urban occupational structure reveals much smaller differentials between both Holland and Trempealeau County in their first two decades and both Holland after 1870 and the cities for which data are available. Excluding Trempealeau County in the 1860's because the

TABLE 52

SUMMARY MEASURES OF OCCUPATIONAL MOBILITY FOR SELECTED COMMUNITIES, 1830–1968

Community	Gross Mobility	Upward Mobility	Downward Mobility	Rural to Urban	Urban to Rural	Minimum Structural Movement	N
Boston, 1830–40	5.5	3.9	1.6	—	—	2.3	128
Boston, 1840–50	3.9	3.9	0.0	—	—	3.9	153
Boston, 1850–60	14.4	12.0	2.4	—	—	9.6	125
Poughkeepsie, 1850–60	13.5	11.0	2.5	—	—	8.6	1168
Poughkeepsie, 1860–70	14.6	11.9	2.7	—	—	9.2	1773
Poughkeepsie, 1870–80	11.6	8.5	3.1	—	—	5.5	2527
Atlanta, 1870–80	10.1	8.1	2.0	—	—	6.0	248
Boston, 1880–90	12.0	7.4	4.6	—	—	2.7	543
Omaha, 1880–91	9.9	9.1	0.8	—	—	8.4	395
Omaha, 1900–11	16.8	13.2	3.6	—	—	9.7	310
Los Angeles, 1910–20	14.1	6.0	8.0	—	—	2.0	249
Boston, 1910–20	17.2	13.3	3.9	—	—	9.4	413
Norristown, 1910–20	8.2	5.5	2.7	—	—	2.8	3905
Norristown, 1920–30	9.2	7.0	2.2	—	—	4.7	3800
Boston, 1930–40	12.8	7.1	5.8	—	—	1.3	467
Norristown, 1930–40	12.3	6.9	5.4	—	—	1.5	4535
Norristown, 1940–50	11.9	7.2	4.6	—	—	2.6	4860
Boston, 1958–68	13.0	8.8	4.3	—	—	4.5	399
Trempealeau County, 1860–70 (All types of movement)	43.5	21.4	6.0	6.5	9.5	23.8	168
Trempealeau County, 1860–70 (Upward and downward mobility within the urban and rural occupational hierarchies)	32.6	25.5	7.1	—	—	18.4	141

TABLE 52 (Continued)

Community	Gross Mobility	Upward Mobility	Downward Mobility	Rural to Urban	Urban to Rural	Minimum Structural Movement	N
Trempealeau County, 1860–70 (Movement within the urban occupational structure only)	22.7	0.0	22.7	—	—	22.7	22
Trempealeau County, 1870–80 (All types of movement)	38.2	24.2	4.1	4.9	4.9	21.4	687
Trempealeau County, 1870–80 (Upward and downward mobility within the urban and rural occupational hierarchies)	31.3	26.8	4.5	—	—	22.3	619
Trempealeau County, 1870–80 (Movement within the urban occupational structure only)	21.5	16.9	4.6	—	—	12.3	65
Holland, 1850–60 (All types of movement)	64.4	33.0	1.8	1.5	28.5	48.4	337
Holland, 1850–60 (Upward and downward mobility within the urban and rural occupational hierarchies)	49.6	47.0	2.5	—	—	44.5	236
Holland, 1850–60 (Movement within the urban occupational structure only)	18.9	17.6	1.4	—	—	16.2	74
Holland, 1860–70 (All types of movement)	39.6	26.3	1.1	7.9	4.3	28.7	631
Holland, 1860–70 (Upward and downward mobility within the urban and rural occupational hierarchies)	31.2	30.0	1.3	—	—	28.7	554

Holland, 1860–70 (Movement within the urban occupational structure only)	19.4	17.4	2.1	—	—	15.3	144
Holland, 1870–80 (All types of movement)	21.2	7.2	4.1	4.2	5.6	5.1	801
Holland, 1870–80 (Upward and downward mobility within the urban and rural occupational hierarchies)	12.6	8.0	4.6	—	—	3.5	722
Holland, 1870–80 (Movement within the urban occupational structure only)	23.1	15.8	7.3	—	—	8.5	260
Holland, 1880–94 (All types of movement)	19.6	5.2	6.9	6.5	1.0	5.6	306
Holland, 1880–94 (Movement within the urban occupational structure only)	13.6	5.9	7.7	—	—	1.8	272

Source: Data for Boston, 1830–1860 are from Knights, 1971: pp. 96–102; Poughkeepsie Mobility Study made available by Clyde Griffin and cited in Thernstrom, 1973: pp. 200–213; Boston data after 1880 from Thernstrom, 1973: p. 234; Atlanta from Hopkins, 1968: p. 234; Omaha from Chudacoff, 1972: pp. 96–110; Los Angeles from Michael Hanson, "Occupational Mobility and Persistence in Los Angeles, 1910–1930," unpublished seminar paper, U.C.L.A., 1970, cited in Thernstrom, 1973: p. 234; Norristown from Goldstein, 1958: pp. 160–95; Trempealeau County from Curti, 1959: pp. 115–258. Data have been recomputed by the author for purposes of this study.

sample is so small (32), gross mobility exceeded 18 per cent
for both Holland in the first two decades and Trempealeau
County in the 1870's. With only the exception of Holland
in the 1870's, rates for the other communities never topped
18 per cent.

In addition to greater gross mobility, residents of newly
established communities also experienced greater opportunity for upward mobility than did those of older areas. Upward rates of movement in both Holland and Trempealeau
County ranged between 20 and 50 per cent in the first two
decades of settlement when upward mobility is based either
on a matrix including those moving across the agricultural/
non-agricultural line or just in one including those remaining
in either the urban or rural occupational hierarchies. On the
other hand, upward movement never surpassed 14 per cent
for any of the cities or Holland after 1870. Again when movement only with the urban occupational categories is considered, the differentials are much smaller. For Holland between
1850 and 1870 and Trempealeau County rates of upward
mobility hovered around 17 per cent while, with the exception of Holland in the 1870's (15.8 per cent), rates of upward
movement in the other communities ranged between 3.9 and
13.3 per cent. By contrast, downward mobility did not vary
among types of communities. Excluding downward movement within the urban occupational structure of Trempealeau
County in the 1860's because of the small size of its sample,
all other rates fell within a range of 0–8 per cent and reveal
no distinct patterns.

Greater changes in the occupational structure of these
newly established communities account most fully for the
higher rates of gross and upward mobility. Although data
on the redistribution of occupations within the labor forces
for these other communities are not available, figures for
minimum structural movement or the amount of mobility
attributable to structural changes based on the mobility matrix are available.[3] When computed from a mobility matrix

---

[3] Although structural change measured on the basis of the entire labor force
would be a better measure than minimum structural movement since the former
includes the effects of migration and net-natural processes on the labor force, there
is justification for using the latter. Both seem to be highly interrelated; in Holland
both moved in the same direction from decade to decade.

including either all types of movement or only mobility within the non-agricultural and agricultural structures, minimum structural movement never fell below 18 per cent in each of the first two decades of the two newly established communities and never topped 10 per cent in either Holland after 1870 or any of the other cities. Although revealing smaller differentials focusing on only the urban occupational hierarchy further indicates greater structural change in Holland and Trempealeau County with minimum structural movement always surpassing 12 per cent.

In summary, comparing the results of mobility in the Holland community with those from other studies clearly indicates that newly settled frontier communities experienced far higher rates of movement and greater opportunity for upward mobility than did older more urban areas. That these differentials were smallest when only movement within the urban occupational hierarchy is considered further indicates that most of the additional movement in newly settled communities took place within the agricultural occupational labor force. These differentials in rates of mobility, moreover, can be traced to the greater structural changes occurring in newly settled communities than in older ones. Since these differentials were greatest when changes in both the urban and rural occupational structures were calculated they indicate that changes in the agricultural labor force associated with the clearing and settling of land provided the greatest impetus for occupational movement in these newly settled communities. More generally these findings indicate that the establishment and early development of communities offered greater inducements to occupational mobility than did urbanization and industrialization.

Although agricultural development in new communities appears to have provided greater opportunity than urbanization and industrialization, a comparison of rates of upward mobility of both blue-collar and rural workers between Holland and the various urban communities suggests the existence of a more open occupational structure within the urban as well as the rural sectors of newly established communities. Rates of blue-collar movement into the white-collar category in the first two decades of the Holland community's existence were on the average higher than those for urban areas (see table 53). In both of these decades over 20 per cent of the blue-collar workers remaining within the urban occupational structure entered white-collar positions. By contrast in only three of the eighteen decades for which data are available for urban areas and only one of the two time periods after 1870 in Holland did movement surpass 20 per cent. Furthermore, that over a third of all blue-collar workers in Holland between 1850 and 1880 became either white-collar workers or farm operators and over 70 per cent of the rural workers became farm operators between 1850 and 1870 further indicates that newer communities provided greater opportunity for those at the bottom than did older areas.[4]

Thus far this analysis has pointed to the differences in the rates of change in the occupational structures between newly settled communities and older ones in accounting for differences in the rates of mobility of these communities. In order to understand further the relationship between occupational mobility and structural change, rates of occupational movement will be correlated with rates of structural change for all communities. In this analysis, data from Holland and Trempealeau County will be from mobility matrices based on the urban occupational structure only and that from Trempealeau County in the 1860's will be omitted because of the small size of the sample.

Pearson's *r* indicates a strong relationship of .66 between minimum structural movement and gross occupational mobility. Perhaps more importantly, the relationship between minimum structural movement and upward mobility is .92. This suggests, although both types of mobility are strongly related to structural change, that the opportunity for upward movement has been more closely tied to structural change that has gross mobility and emphasizes the importance of

---

[4] These findings suggest a modification of Thernstrom's conclusion that there was no great variation in patterns of intra-generational mobility among communities and that city size did not alter this pattern. His omission of newly settled rural areas from his comparison of nineteenth-century communities accounts for different conclusions regarding variations in intra-generational mobility among communities. Thernstrom, 1973: pp. 232–236. In addition, Palmer, 1954: pp. 35–38, suggests that there are variations in labor mobility among cities. However, her study does not deal directly with vertical occupational mobility and is concerned only with individuals changing employers. Thus it does not speak directly to the issue at hand.

TABLE 53

DECADAL MOBILITY RATES OF BLUE-COLLAR WORKERS IN
SELECTED COMMUNITIES, 1830–1968

	Per Cent Blue-collar Workers Becoming White-collar Workers	N
Boston, 1830–40	9	58
Boston, 1840–50	10	60
Boston, 1850–60	18	83
Poughkeepsie, 1850–60	17	758
Poughkeepsie, 1860–70	18	1172
Poughkeepsie, 1870–80	13	1661
Atlanta, 1870–80	10	182
Boston, 1880–90	12	334
Omaha, 1880–91	21	255
Omaha, 1900–11	23	180
Boston, 1910–20	22	248
Los Angeles, 1910–20	16	95
Norristown, 1910–20	8	2745
Norristown, 1920–30	10	2715
Boston, 1930–40	11	301
Norristown, 1930–40	10	3145
Norristown, 1940–50	11	3555
Boston, 1958–68	17	206
Holland, 1850–60	21	62
Holland, 1860–70	24	105
Holland, 1870–80	25	167
Holland, 1880–94	9	174

Source: See note to table 52 for sources. Data for Holland
are based on those remaining within the urban occupational
structure only.

structural change for increasing opportunity in American history. However, that minimum structural movement ignores the effects of migration and net-natural processes on the occupational structure and consequently may not be the best measure of structural change necessitates some caution regarding this conclusion. Yet, the strong correlations do suggest a relationship and further point out the need for other studies of community mobility to be sensitive to changes taking place within the entire occupational structure in order to obtain a clearer understanding of the mobility process.

These findings also have broader implications for understanding the mobility process and opportunity in the Western World in the nineteenth century. One of the most important

studies of social mobility in the post-World War II period
and one of the few to theorize implicitly on nineteenth-century mobility has been Lipset and Bendix's *Social Mobility in
Industrial Society*. Arguing that widespread social mobility occurs concomitantly with the processes of urbanization, industrialization, and bureaucratization, Lipset and Bendix posit
that there is no difference in the rate of mobility among
industrialized nations and consequently that the United
States does not differ substantially from the nations of Western Europe in this respect. In addition, they indicate that
this pattern of equal mobility held for the nineteenth century,
although not offering any evidence to support that proposi-
tion. Thus they suggest that the reason many have believed
that America is the land of opportunity *vis-à-vis* Europe is
due to the ideology of success that pervades the American
ethos.[5]

The Holland study, while not challenging Lipset and Bendix's findings about comparable rates of mobility among
industrialized nations in the twentieth century, does raise
questions about their inferences concerning the nineteenth
century and the impact of urbanization, industrialization, and
bureaucratization on the mobility process. The findings from
the Holland community suggest that Lipset and Bendix over-
look an important dynamic factor in their pronouncements
on the nineteenth century. That is, they fail to take into consideration the structural changes brought about by the westward movement and the subsequent clearing of land and
the establishing of towns. In the Holland community, these
changes both gave a greater impetus to occupational movement than did the subsequent changes brought by industrialization and the development of the city of Holland and gener-
ated higher levels of mobility than did nineteenth- and
twentieth-century cities. Given the importance of the
westward movement in nineteenth-century America and the
pattern of mobility in the Holland community, it seems more
likely than not that the United States offered greater opportu-

---

[5] Lipset and Bendix, 1964: p. 34. In addition, a study of Bochum in the Ruhr
during the last two decades of the nineteenth century indicates that there was far
less intra-generational occupational mobility in Germany than in the United States.
See Crew, 1973: pp. 52–53.

nity than did Europe in the nineteenth century.[6] This may also explain why the American ideology, partly based upon a comparison with Europe, gained such popularity in the nineteenth century. This is not to imply that the American social structure measured up to the ideals of the American dream but merely to argue that this view was strengthened in the public mind because America with its frontier provided greater promises and more examples of men getting ahead than did Europe.

---

[6] A study of inter-generational occupational mobility in Copenhagen from 1850 to 1950 indicates little change in the amount of mobility in the last hundred years. These results would seem to support Lipset and Bendix's inferences about comparable rates of mobility in the nineteenth century. However, comparing the data for Copenhagen with that of nineteenth-century American cities still overlooks the high rates of occupational mobility induced by structural changes resulting from the westward movement and subsequent clearing of land and the establishment of new communities. See Rishøj, 1971: pp. 135–140.

Bibliography

Manuscripts

Census of the State of Michigan, 1894: Population, Michigan State Archives.
Eighth Census of the United States, 1860: Census of Agriculture, Michigan State Archives.
Eighth Census of the United States, 1860: Manufacturers of the United States, Michigan State Archives.
Eighth Census of the United States, 1860: Population of the United States (microfilmed), Michigan State Library.
Emigration Records, The Netherlands, 1848–1876, Calvin College, Heritage Hall Collection.
Ninth Census of the United States, 1870: Census of Agriculture, Michigan State Archives.
Ninth Census of the United States, 1870: Manufacturers of the United States, Michigan State Archives.
Ninth Census of the United States, 1870: Population of the United States (microfilmed), Michigan State Library.
Seventh Census of the United States, 1850: Census of Agriculture, Michigan State Archives.
Seventh Census of the United States, 1850: Manufacturers of the United States, Michigan State Archives.
Seventh Census of the United States, 1850: Population of the United States (microfilmed), Michigan State Library.
Tenth Census of the United States, 1880: Census of Agriculture, Michigan State Archives.
Tenth Census of the United States, 1880: Special Census of Manufacturers, Michigan State Archives.
Tenth Census of the United States, 1880: Population of the United States (microfilmed), Michigan State Library.

Printed Documents

Michigan Department of State. 1855. *Census & Statistics of the State of Michigan, 1854* (Lansing, Mich.).
Michigan Department of State. 1865. *Census & Statistics of the State of Michigan, 1864* (Lansing, Mich.).
Michigan Department of State. 1875. *Census of the State of Michigan, 1874* (Lansing, Mich.).
Michigan Department of State. 1885. *Census of the State of Michigan, 1884: Agriculture and Manufactories* (2V., Lansing, Mich.).
Michigan Department of State. 1895. *Census of the State of Michigan, 1894: Agriculture, Manufactories, Mines and Fisheries* (2V., Lansing, Mich.).
U.S. Department of Commerce, Bureau of the Census. 1966. *Historical Statistics of the United States, Colonial Times to 1957* (Washington, D.C.).

147

Memoirs and Minutes

CLASSIS HOLLAND. 1943. *Minutes, 1848–1858,* trans. by a joint committee of the Christian Reformed Church and the Reformed Church in America (Grand Rapids, Mich.).
LUCAS, HENRY S., ed. 1955. *Dutch Immigrant Memoirs and Related Writings* (2v., Seattle).

Newspaper

Holland Evening Sentinel, 1871–1895.

Books and Articles

BABCOCK, HENDRICK C. 1941. *The Scandinavian Element in the United States* (Urbana, Ill.).
BARR, ALWYN. 1970. "Occupational and Geographic Mobility in San Antonio, 1870–1900." *Social Science Quarterly* 51: pp. 396–403.
BERGMAN, LEOLA NELSON. 1958. *Americans From Norway* (Philadelphia).
BLALOCK, HUBERT M., JR. 1960. *Social Statistics* (New York, Toronto and London).
BLAU, PETER M., and OTIS DUDLEY DUNCAN. 1967. *The American Occupational Structure* (New York).
BLUMIN, STUART. 1968. "The Historical Study of Vertical Mobility." *Historical Methods Newsletter* 1: pp. 1–13.
———— 1969. "Mobility and Change in Ante-Bellum Philadelphia." In: Stephan Thernstrom and Richard Sennett, eds., *Nineteenth-Century Cities: Essays in the New Urban History* (New Haven and London).
BOGUE, ALLAN G. 1963. *From Prairie to Corn Belt: Farming on the Illinois and Iowa Prairies in the Nineteenth Century* (Chicago).
BOWERS, WILLIAM L. 1960. "Crawford Township, 1850–70: A Population Study of a Pioneer Community." *Iowa Jour. History* 58: pp. 1–30.
CAWELTI, JOHN G. 1965. *Apostles of the Self-Made Man* (Chicago and London).
CHUDACOFF, HOWARD P. 1972. *Mobile Americans: Residential and Social Mobility in Omaha, 1880–1920* (New York).
COLEMAN, PETER J. 1962. "Restless Grant County: Americans on the Move." *Wisconsin Mag. of History* 66: pp. 16–20.
CREW, DAVID. 1973. "Definitions of Modernity: Social Mobility in a German Town, 1880–1901." *Jour. Social History* 7: pp. 51–74.
CURTI, MERLE. 1959. *The Making of an American Community: A Case Study of Democracy in a Frontier Community* (Stanford, California).
DEGLER, CARL N. 1962. *Out of Our Past: The Forces That Shaped Modern America* (New York and Evanston).
DUNCAN, OTIS DUDLEY. 1966. "Methodological Issues in the Analysis of Social Mobility." In: Neil J. Smelser and Seymour Martin Lipset, eds., *Social Structure and Mobility in Economic Development* (Chicago), pp. 51–97.
DYKSTRA, ROBERT R. 1971. Review of *Nineteenth-Century Cities: Essays in the New Urban History,* by Stephan Thernstrom and Richard Sennett, eds. *Jour. Social History* 5: p. 123.
FAUST, ALBERT. 1909. *The German Element in the United States* (Boston).
GATES, PAUL W. 1957. "Frontier Estate Builders and Farm Laborers." In: Walker D. Wyman and C. B. Kroeber, eds., *The Frontier in Perspective* (Madison, Wis.), pp. 144–163.
GOLDSTEIN, SIDNEY. 1955. "Migration and Occupational Mobility in Norristown, Pennsylvania." *Amer. Sociol. Rev.* 20: pp. 402–408.

———— 1958. *Patterns of Mobility, 1910–1950: The Norristown Study* (Philadelphia).

GREGORY, FRANCIS W., and IRENE D. NEU. 1962. "The American Industrial Elite in the 1870s: Their Social Origins." In: William Miller, ed., *Men in Business: Essays on the Historical Role of the Entrepreneur* (New York), pp. 193–211.

GREVEN, PHILLIP J., JR. 1970. *Four Generations: Population, Land, and Family in Colonial Andover, Massachusetts* (Ithaca).

GRIFFIN, CLYDE. 1970. "Making It in America: Social Mobility in Mid-Nineteenth Century Poughkeepsie." *New York History* **51**: pp. 479–499.

———— 1972. "Occupational Mobility in Nineteenth-Century America: Problems and Possibilities." *Jour. Social History* **5**: pp. 310–330.

HANDLIN, OSCAR. 1951. *The Uprooted: The Epic Story of the Great Migrations that Made the American People* (New York).

HARRIS, P. M. G. 1969. "The Social Origins of American Leaders: The Demographic Foundations." *Perspectives in Amer. History* **3**: pp. 159–344.

HOPKINS, RICHARD J. 1968 "Occupational and Geographic Mobility in Atlanta, 1870–1896." *Jour. Southern History* **34**: pp. 200–213.

———— 1972. "Status, Mobility, and the Dimensions of Change in a Southern City: Atlanta, 1870–1910." In: Kenneth T. Jackson and Stanley K. Schultz, eds., *Cities in American History* (New York), pp. 216–231.

HYMA, ALBERT. 1947. *Albertus C. Van Raalte and His Dutch Settlement in the United States* (Grand Rapids, Mich.).

JACKSON, ELTON F., and HARRY J. CROCKETT. 1964. "Occupational Mobility in the United States: A Point Estimate and Trend Comparison." *Amer. Sociol. Rev.* **29**: pp. 5–16.

JOHANSEN, DOROTHY O. 1967. "A Working Hypothesis for the Study of Migration." *Pacific Hist. Rev.* **36**: pp. 1–12.

JOHNSON, HILDEGARD BINDER. 1951. "The Location of the German Immigrants in the Middle West." *Annals Assoc. Amer. Geographers* **61**: pp. 1–41.

KATZ, MICHAEL B. 1972. "Occupational Classification in History." *Jour. Interdisciplinary History* **3**: pp. 63–88.

KNIGHTS, PETER R. 1971. *The Plain People of Boston, 1830–60: A Study in City Growth* (New York).

LAMPARD, ERIC E. 1965. "Historical Aspects of Urbanization." In: Phillip M. Hauser and Leo F. Schnore, eds., *The Study of Urbanization* (New York), pp. 519–554.

LENSKI, GERHARD E. 1958. "Trends in Inter-Generational Mobility in the United States." *Amer. Sociol. Rev.* **23**: pp. 514–523.

———— 1966. *Power and Privilege: A Theory of Social Stratification* (New York).

LIPSET, SEYMOUR MARTIN, and REINHARD BENDIX, ed. 1953. *Class, Status, and Power* (Glencoe, Illinois).

———— 1964. *Social Mobility in Industrial Society* (Berkeley and Los Angeles).

LOWRY, IRA S. 1966. *Migration and Metropolitan Growth: Two Analytical Models* (San Francisco).

LUCAS, HENRY S. 1955. *Netherlanders in America: Dutch Immigration to the United States and Canada, 1789–1950* (Ann Arbor).

MALIN, JAMES C. 1935. "The Turnover of Farm Population in Kansas." *Kansas Hist. Quart.* **4**: pp. 339–372.

MILLER, S. M. 1960. "Comparative Social Mobility: A Trend Report and Bibliography." *Current Sociology* **9**, 1: pp. 1–89.

MILLER WILLIAM. 1949. "American Historians and the Business Elite." *Jour. Econ. History* **9**: pp. 184–208.

———— 1962. "The Recruitment of the American Business Elite." In: William Miller, ed., *Men in Business: Essays on the Historical Role of the Entrepreneur* (New York), pp. 329–358.

MITCHELL, G. A. 1893. "City of Holland." In: Hiram Potts, ed., *A Complete Historical,*

Statistical, Biographical, and Geographical Compendium of Ottawa County's Public and Private Interests and Institutions (2 v., Grand Haven, Mich.) **1:** pp. 157–203.

MORRISON, PETER A. 1970. "Urban Growth, New Cities, and 'The Population Problem.' " Rand Corporation Paper #P-4515–1.

NYHOLM, PAUL C. 1963. *The Americanization of the Danish Lutheran Church in America: A Study in Immigrant History* (Copenhagen).

PALMER, GLADYS L. 1954. *Labor Mobility in Six Cities: A Report on the Survey of Patterns and Factors in Labor Mobility, 1940–1950* (New York).

PESSEN, EDWARD. 1971. "The Egalitarian Myth and the American Social Reality: Wealth, Mobility, and Equality in the 'Era of the Common Man.' " *Amer. Hist. Rev.* **76:** pp. 989–1034.

PIETERS, ALIEDA J. 1923. *A Dutch Settlement in Michigan* (Grand Rapids, Mich.).

POTTS, HIRAM A., ed. 1893. *A Complete Historical, Statistical, Biographical, and Geographical Compendium of Ottawa County's Public and Private Interests and Institutions* (2 v., Grand Haven, Mich.).

QUALEY, CARLTON C. 1938. *Norwegian Settlement in the United States* (Northfield, Minn.).

RISHØJ, TOM. 1971. "Metropolitan Social Mobility 1850–1950: The Case of Copenhagen." *Quality and Quantity* **5:** pp. 131–140.

ROBBINS, WILLIAM G. 1970. "Opportunity and Persistence in the Pacific Northwest: A Quantitative Study of Early Rosburg, Oregon." *Pacific Hist. Rev.* **39:** pp. 279–296.

ROGOFF, NATALIE. 1953. *Recent Trends in Occupational Mobility* (New York).

SCHNORE, LEO F. 1959. "Social Mobility in Demographic Perspective." In: Leo F. Schnore, ed., *The Urban Scene: Human Ecology and Demography* (New York), pp. 44–76.

SMELSER, NEIL J., and SEYMOUR MARTIN LIPSET. 1966. *Social Structure and Mobility in Economic Development* (Chicago).

SMITH, PAGE. 1966. *As A City Upon a Hill: The Town in American History* (New York).

STEPHENSON, GEORGE M. 1964. *A History of American Immigration, 1820–1924* (New York).

THERNSTROM, STEPHAN. 1964. *Poverty and Progress: Social Mobility in a Nineteenth Century City* (Cambridge, Mass.).

——— 1973. *The Other Bostonians: Poverty and Progress in the American Metropolis, 1880–1970* (Cambridge, Mass.).

THRONE, MILDRED. 1959. "A Population Study of an Iowa County in 1850." *Iowa Jour. History* **57:** pp. 305–330.

VANDERVEEN, ENGBERTUS. 1911. *Life History and Reminiscences of Engbertus VanderVeen* (Holland, Mich.).

VAN KOEVERING, ADRIAN. n.d. *The Dutch Colonial Pioneers of Western Michigan: The Story of a Mass Movement of Nineteenth Century Pilgrims* (Zeeland, Mich.).

WABEKE, BERTUS HARRY. 1944. *Dutch Emigration to North America: 1624–1860* (New York).

WESTOFF, CHARLES F., MARVIN BRESSLER, and PHILLIP SAGI. 1960. "The Concept of Social Mobility: An Empirical Inquiry." *Amer. Sociol. Rev.* **25:** pp. 375–385.

WINCHESTER, IAN. 1970. "The Linkage of Historical Records by Man and Computer: Techniques and Problems." *Jour. Interdisciplinary History* **1:** pp. 107–124.

WORTHMAN, PAUL B. 1971. "Working Class Mobility in Birmingham, Alabama, 1880–1914." In: Tamara K. Hareven, ed. *Anonymous Americans: Explorations in Nineteenth Century Social History* (Englewood Cliffs, N.J.).

WYLLIE, IRWIN G. 1954. *The Self-Made Man in America: The Myth of Rags to Riches* (New York and London).

APPENDIX I

Components of Change in the Labor
Force of the Holland Community
by Occupation and Decade,
1850–1880

TABLE 54

Components of Change in the Labor Force of the Holland Community, 1850–1860 (based on 1860 Labor Force)

Occupation	Net-Migration		Net Occupational Mobility		Net Natural Processes	
	No.	%	No.	%	No.	%
White-collar	31	52.2	13	19.4	0	0.0
Professionals	7	35.0	3	15.0	0	0.0
Big Businessmen[a]	3	42.9	3	42.9	0	0.0
Small Businessmen[b]	13	44.8	5	17.2	0	0.0
Clerical & Sales	8	72.7	2	18.2	0	0.0
Blue-collar	82	35.0	-104	-44.4	-25	-10.7
Skilled Workers	57	45.6	-9	-7.2	-3	-2.4
Semiskilled Workers	28	77.8	5	13.9	2	5.6
Unskilled Workers	-3	-4.1	-100	-137.0	-24	-32.9
Farm Operators	117	36.4	150	46.7	4	1.2
Farmers (over $5,000)	0	0.0	0	0.0	0	0.0
Farmers ($1,001–$5,000)	42	36.5	62	53.9	3	2.6
Farmers ($501–$1,000)	45	33.8	75	54.9	5	3.8
Farmers ($500 & under)	30	41.1	13	17.8	-4	-5.5
Rural Workers	213	52.1	-59	-14.4	47	11.5
Gardeners	3	37.5	2	25.0	1	12.5
Tenants & Sharecroppers[c]	0	0.0	0	0.0	0	0.0
"Farmers without Farms"	138	49.8	-65	-23.5	9	3.2
Farm Laborers	72	58.1	4	3.2	37	29.8

[a]This category includes businessmen listed in the industrial census as being the owners or partners in a concern with a capitalization in excess of $1,000.

[b]This category includes all those listed in the general census as public officials, merchants, proprietors, and managers, and who are not listed in the industrial census as being the owners or partners in a concern with a capitalization of $1,000 or more.

[c]None listed in either the census of 1850 or 1860.

TABLE 55

Components of Change in the Labor Force of the Holland Community, 1860–1870 (Based on 1870 Labor Force)

Occupation	Net-Migration		Net Occupational Mobility		Net Natural Processes	
	No.	%	No.	%	No.	%
White-collar	91	44.6	40	19.6	6	2.9
Professional	21	58.3	-4	-11.1	-1	-2.8
Big Businessmen[a]	10	29.4	16	47.1	1	3.0
Small Businessmen[b]	54	48.6	25	22.5	3	2.7
Clerical & Sales	6	26.1	3	13.0	3	13.0
Blue-collar	300	58.7	-17	-3.3	-6	-1.2
Skilled Workers	109	52.4	-15	-7.2	-11	-5.3
Semiskilled Workers	50	50.5	6	11.5	7	7.1
Unskilled Workers	141	69.1	-8	-3.9	-2	-1.0
Farm Operators	202	31.1	141	21.7	-15	-2.3
Farmers (over $5000)	3	11.5	23	88.5	0	0.0
Farmers ($1001–$5000)	100	24.0	204	49.0	-3	-0.7
Farmers ($501–$1000)	79	50.6	-48	-30.8	-8	-5.1
Farmers ($500 & under)	20	39.2	-38	-74.4	-4	-7.8
Rural Workers	-74	-49.7	-164	-110.1	-22	-14.8
Gardeners	-1	-12.5	0	0.0	0	0.0
Tenants & Sharecroppers[c]	0	0.0	0	0.0	0	0.0
"Farmers without Farms"	-54	-60.7	-119	-134.7	-15	-16.9
Farm Laborers	-19	-35.8	-45	-84.9	-7	-13.2

[a] This category includes businessmen listed in the industrial census as being the owners or partners in a concern with a capitalization in excess of $1,000.

[b] This category includes all those listed in the general census as public officials, merchants, proprietors, and managers, and who are not listed in the industrial census as being the owners or partners in a concern with a capitalization of $1,000 or more.

[c] None listed in either the census of 1860 or 1870.

TABLE 56
COMPONENTS OF CHANGE IN THE LABOR FORCE OF THE HOLLAND COMMUNITY, 1870–1880 (BASED ON 1880 LABOR FORCE)

Occupation	Net-Migration		Net Occupational Mobility		Net Natural Processes	
	No.	%	No.	%	No.	%
White-collar	43	13.6	25	7.9	44	13.9
Professional	15	23.4	7	10.9	6	9.4
Big Businessmen [a]	7	15.9	4	9.1	-1	-2.3
Small Businessmen [b]	10	6.7	14	9.3	15	10.0
Clerical & Sales	11	19.0	0	0.0	24	41.4
Blue-collar	138	20.4	-36	-5.3	65	9.6
Skilled Workers	52	18.9	1	0.4	14	5.1
Semiskilled Workers	118	41.0	4	1.4	67	23.3
Unskilled Workers	-32	-27.8	-41	-35.7	-16	-13.9
Farm Operators	91	13.2	16	2.3	-66	-9.6
Farmers (over $5000)	2	3.3	36	59.0	-3	-4.9
Farmers ($1001-$5000)	72	15.6	14	3.0	-40	-8.7
Farmers ($501-$1000)	16	12.4	-27	-20.9	-16	-12.4
Farmers ($500 & under)	1	2.6	-7	-18.4	-7	-18.4
Rural Workers	85	19.7	5	1.2	203	47.0
Gardeners	-1	-20.0	0	0.0	-1	-20.0
Tenants & Sharecroppers [c]	12	63.2	4	21.1	3	15.8
"Farmers without Farms"	13	7.6	-4	-2.3	74	43.0
Farm Laborers	61	25.8	-5	-2.1	127	53.8

[a] This category includes businessmen listed in the industrial census as being the owners or partners in a concern with a capitalization in excess of $1,000.

[b] This category includes all those listed in the general census as public officials, merchants, proprietors, and managers, and who are not listed in the industrial census as being the owners or partners in a concern with a capitalization of $1,000 or more.

[c] None listed in either the census of 1870.

APPENDIX II

Migration Rates for the Holland Community by Occupation and Decade, 1850–1880

TABLE 57

Migration Rates for the Holland Community, 1850–1860

Occupation	In-Migration		Out-Migration		Net-Migration	
	No.	%	No.	%	No.	%
White-collar	40	59.7	9	39.1	31	49.2
Professional	13	65.0	6	60.0	7	35.0
Big Businessmen	3	42.9	0	0.0	3	42.9
Small Businessmen	15	51.7	2	18.2	13	44.8
Clerical & Sales	9	81.8	1	100.0	8	72.7
Blue-collar	166	70.9	84	29.1	82	35.0
Skilled Workers	82	65.6	25	31.3	57	45.6
Semiskilled Workers	28	77.8	0	0.0	28	77.8
Unskilled Workers	56	76.7	59	29.5	−3	−4.1
Farm Operators	128	39.9	11	22.0	117	36.4
Farmers (over $5000)	0	0.0	0	0.0	0	0.0
Farmers ($1001–$5000)	43	37.4	1	12.5	42	36.5
Farmers ($501–$1000)	47	35.3	2	25.0	45	33.8
Farmers ($500 & under)	38	52.1	8	23.5	30	41.1
Rural Workers	256	62.6	43	20.7	213	52.1
Gardeners	5	62.5	2	100.0	3	37.5
Tenants & Sharecroppers*	0	0.0	0	0.0	0	0.0
"Farmers without Farms"	175	63.2	37	18.0	138	49.8
Farm Laborers	76	61.3	4	27.5	72	58.1
Totals	590	57.2	147	26.2	443	43.0

* None listed in either the census of 1850 or 1860.

TABLE 58
Migration Rates for the Holland Community, 1860–1870

Occupation	In-Migration		Out-Migration		Net-Migration	
	No.	%	No.	%	No.	%
White-collar	109	53.4	18	26.9	91	44.6
Professionals	27	75.0	6	30.0	21	58.3
Big Businessmen	10	29.4	0	0.0	10	29.4
Small Businessmen	61	55.0	7	24.1	54	48.6
Clerical & Sales	11	47.8	5	45.5	6	26.1
Blue-collar	381	74.6	81	34.6	300	58.7
Skilled Workers	147	70.7	38	30.4	109	52.4
Semiskilled Workers	63	63.6	13	36.1	50	50.5
Unskilled Workers	171	83.8	30	41.1	141	69.1
Farm Operators	241	37.1	39	12.1	202	31.1
Farmers (over $5000)	3	11.5	0	0.0	3	11.5
Farmers ($1001–$5000)	119	28.6	19	16.5	100	24.0
Farmers ($501–$1000)	88	56.4	9	6.8	79	50.6
Farmers (under $500)	31	60.8	11	15.1	20	39.2
Rural Workers	83	55.7	157	38.4	−74	−49.7
Gardeners	2	28.6	3	37.5	−1	−12.5
Tenants & Sharecroppers*	0	0.0	0	0.0	0	0.0
"Farmers without Farms"	42	47.2	96	34.7	−54	−60.7
Farm Laborers	39	73.6	58	46.8	−19	−37.7
Total	814	53.8	295	28.7	519	34.3

* None listed in either the census of 1860 or 1870.

TABLE 59

Migration Rates for the Holland Community, 1870–1880

Occupation	In-Migration		Out-Migration		Net-Migration	
	No.	%	No.	%	No.	%
White-collar	113	35.8	70	34.3	43	13.6
Professional	34	53.1	19	52.8	15	23.4
Big Businessmen	9	20.5	2	5.9	7	15.9
Small Businessmen	49	32.7	39	35.1	10	6.7
Clerical & Sales	21	36.2	10	43.5	11	19.0
Blue-collar	366	54.0	228	44.6	138	20.4
Skilled Workers	136	49.5	84	40.4	52	18.9
Semiskilled Workers	157	54.5	39	39.4	118	41.0
Unskilled Workers	73	63.5	105	51.5	−32	−27.8
Farm Operators	183	26.5	92	14.2	91	13.2
Farmers (over $5000)	3	4.9	1	3.8	2	3.3
Farmers ($1001–$5000)	108	23.4	36	8.7	72	15.6
Farmers ($501–$1000)	55	42.6	39	25.0	16	12.4
Farmers ($500 & under)	17	44.7	16	31.4	1	2.6
Rural Workers	161	37.3	76	51.0	85	19.7
Gardeners	2	40.0	3	42.9	−1	−20.0
Tenants & Sharecroppers*	12	63.2	0	0.0	12	63.2
"Farmers without Farms"	55	32.0	42	47.2	13	7.6
Farm Laborers	92	39.0	31	58.5	61	25.8
Totals	823	38.9	466	30.8	357	16.9

* None listed in the census of 1870.

Index

Atlanta, Ga., 8

Belgian revolution of 1830, 17–18
Bendix, Reinhard, 133, 144
Birmingham, Ala., 8
Blau, Peter M., 131
Blumin, Stuart, 6–7, 59
Boston, 7
Bressler, Marvin, 59, 62
Brummelkamp, Antonie, 19, 20

Chudacoff, Howard, 8
Curti, Merle, 6, 37

DeCock, Hendrick C., 17
Duncan, Otis Dudley, 131

"Farmers without farms," 37–38

Galveston, Texas, 8
Gates, Paul, 37
Geographic mobility: and occupational mobility, 48–51, 55–57, 73–74, 130–131; Johansen theory, 10–11. *See also* Migration; Persistence
Goldstein, Sidney, 57
Gregory, Francis W., 1
Griffin, Clyde, 7–8

Handlin, Oscar, 12
Harris, P. M. G., 2, 3
Holland, city of, *see* Holland Community
Holland Community, 10–11, 21–23, 129; agricultural growth, 31–35, 129; economic development, 9–10, 24, 129; ethnic composition, 23–24, 129; impact of transportation improvements on, 25, 30; industrial growth, 24–31, 129; labor force, 23–24, 130; origins, 16, 19, 21; population growth, 9–10, 21–23; representativeness, 9–12; sources, 12–13. *See also* Occupational structure
Holland Township, *see* Holland Community

In-migration, 48–51, 131. *See also* Migration; Geographic mobility

Java, 18, 20
Johansen, Dorothy O., 10–11

Knights, Peter R., 7

Lampard, Eric, 83
Lenski, Gerhard E., 1, 8
Lipset, Seymour Martin, 132–133, 144
Lowry, Ira S., 51

Migration, 10–11, 12; Dutch to Holland Community, 16, 17–20; and economic conditions, 17–19, 20; and religious suppression, 19–20; relationship to occupational mobility, 48–51, 55–57, 73–74, 130–131. *See also* Geographic mobility; In-migration; Net-migration; Out-migration; Persistence
Miller, William, 1
Morrison, Peter A., 51

Net-migration: impact on labor force and occupational structure, 42–43, 44–47, 130–131
Net-natural processes, 40–42; impact on labor force and occupational structure, 42–44, 44–47
Net-occupational mobility: impact on labor force and occupational structure, 40–41, 44–47
Neu, Irene B., 2
Newburyport, Mass., 6
Netherlands: economic conditions, 17–19, 20; religious schism; 16–17, 19
Norristown, 57

Occupation: relationship to wealth, 59–63
Occupational classification, 63
Occupational mobility: and age, 88, 96; comparisons between Holland and

163